Essay Index

9.50

The Procession of Masks

HERBERT S. GORMAN

The Procession of Masks

By

HERBERT SHERMAN GORMAN

Essay Index Reprint Series

Essay Index

 BOOKS FOR LIBRARIES PRESS
FREEPORT, NEW YORK

First Published 1923
Reprinted 1969

STANDARD BOOK NUMBER:
8369-1352-3

LIBRARY OF CONGRESS CATALOG CARD NUMBER:
77-99698

PRINTED IN THE UNITED STATES OF AMERICA

FOR JEAN WRIGHT GORMAN

O delicate and dearly wise,
  Beneath what masks have you not peered
And searched with those great starry eyes
  For issues that we hoped and feared,
And, finding much so dark to me,
  Yet simple as the grass to you,
Uncoiled the tangled mystery
  Until I saw the heart and knew?

CONTENTS

EDWIN ARLINGTON ROBINSON

EDWIN ARLINGTON ROBINSON

I.

S it necessary to affirm that there can be no individualism in art without symbolism? Realist, romanticist, mystic and expressionist alike, they conceal and reveal themselves with the same basic substance. I like to think that all literature is an eternal Noh drama in which the creators advance upon the stage to drum-beats and flute-calls and the deliberate clang of bells, wearing upon their faces the self-carved masks which symbolize the passions and meditations to which they strive to give utterance. Upon each mask is graven the personality of the wearer, a personality that is exaggerated and emphasized in strange ways that the essential subject may be better communicated to the mazed audience so restless with its own perturbations. There are masks that have been terribly grooved and hollowed, masks stained with barbaric colors, and masks fashioned ambiguously fair by subtle and delicate strokes. All of them are twisted, either greatly or slightly, from the truth; there is not a naked face in all literature. " Literature," declared Remy de Gourmont, an exotic dancer with many masks, " . . . is nothing more than the artistic development of the idea, the symbolization of the idea." Accepting this statement, the poetry of Edwin Arlington Robinson awakens the question, what is and has been his idea? What has been the permeating objective of this solitary figure's meditations, adhered to so closely since the publication of that tiny, paper-covered pamphlet, " The Torrent and the Night Before," privately printed in Gardiner, Maine, in 1896? Behind what masks has he set slow and inevitable feet upon the uncrowded stage of American letters?

His entrance was made when the editors of The Yellow Book, The Savoy and their disciples were posturing to bizarre melodies behind bewildering visages, when that master of all masqueraders, Oscar Wilde, had but recently suffered the demolition of his cruelly-carven archaic mask, when American letters were dancing to the pleasurable aspects of Messrs. Stone and Kimball's Chicago Chap Book. It was in the days of Thomas Bailey Aldrich and Richard Watson Gilder. Whatever hedonism there was expressed itself in the neat, vagabondian rhymes of Bliss Carman and Richard Hovey. William Vaughan Moody was the Coming Giant. It is strange to reflect that none of these things influenced Robinson. " Twenty-five years ago," he said to me once, " I was a radical." He passed most of those days at home hammering out the sonnets that went into his first booklet. Certain friends at Harvard (where he never completed his course) knew of him and awaited the revelation. They have waited for a quarter of a century, only to realize that the revelation was before their eyes all the time. It was not to be a sudden pillar of fire; it was the deliberate gesture of granite.

It is a difficult and dangerous undertaking to attempt to lay bare the essential node of Robinson's personality. He is a fatalist and at the same time, I am sure, a Christian. He is an optimist and he is a pessimist. He is a tragedian and he is a humorist. He is a conservative and he is a radical. He is a great revealer and he is the most reticent personage in American letters. Not infrequently he circumscribes a thought as intricately and as ambiguously as Henry James, and he can flash home a system of philosophy in a single line. Two things may assuredly be affirmed: he is an individualist and he is never unhealthy. In certain objective ways and in one or two deeply-veined lodes of mind the mark of New England is upon him; but in vaster, more intricate subjective ways he is simply Anglo-Saxon of no particular section. He can never be dismissed as a regional poet. He undoubtedly lacks Latin fire, and when he is passionate it is with a cerebral consciousness of the devouring flame. In other words, he never tears loose. Even in his early work meditation practically extinguished emotionalism. I don't remember that it has ever been pointed out that in the nineties at Harvard there was a deal of interest in Oriental mysticism, in Hindu philosophy. Might not Robinson have been vaguely colored by this during his formative period? Certainly there are times when he suggests the Indian stoic, the dispassionate and austere cerebralist who sits in meditation before the passing colored pomps of jangling Time.

Still, there *are* passages in Robinson's work, notably in "Lancelot," where emotion bursts forth into an undeniable flower of flame. Even in the shorter poems these sudden flashes are to be found. They become the white-hot cores of the thoughts, the admirable technical twist that plunges the poem into the mind and leaves it there — a burning thing. The tensely-packed thought marches past, beating inexorably upon the brain, and then comes the high gust of pictorial poetry that illuminates the entire pro-

18

ceeding. One needs but two examples to illustrate this superb command of inspiration and technique, this fine marriage of the mind and the emotions. The final stanza of " The Gift of God," for instanc , is a beautiful revelation of this magic. Here we have the worthless son seen through the adoring eyes of the mother.

> She crowns him with her gratefulness,
> And says again that life is good;
> And should the gift of God be less
> In him than in her motherhood,
> His fame, though vague, will not be small,
> As upward through her dream he fares,
> Half clouded with a crimson fall
> Of roses thrown on marble stairs.

And in the concluding lines to " Eros Turannos" the same method is evident.

> Meanwhile we do no harm; for they
>   That with a god have striven,
> Not hearing much of what we say,
>   Take what the god has given;
> Though like waves breaking it may be,
> Or like a changed familiar tree,
> Or like a stairway to the sea
>   Where down the blind are driven.

One can do no more than indicate the essential traits of such a profound and complex personality. And the easiest way to do this is to observe the

masks through whose carved lips Robinson has delivered his comments on life. These masks are
easily distinguishable. They are the Tilbury figures
and kindred imaginary conceptions, the historical
portraits and such personal conclusions as " The
Man Against the Sky " and " The Valley of the
Shadow." Reading the poet's entire work again,
the major fact that stands out is that Robinson has
almost wholly delivered himself through characterizations. The pageant of figures is enormous, beginning with Luke Havergal and John Evereldown,
coming down through Shakespeare and St. Paul and
Rembrandt, to the more recent Avon and Roman
Bartholow. It is astonishing to note the admirable
discretion that Robinson exhibits in his choice of
subjects. His failures are so few and his successes
so many, we may guess, because he attempts nothing
that does not bite at him frantically, that does not
indubitably dissolve into his own mind. There is
Rembrandt, for instance. With the consideration
of Robinson's own life and methods of portraiture
in mind, what better subject could have been chosen?
As the Flemish master was a genius of portraiture,
faces in a " golden shadow," so is Robinson a genius
in the meticulous presentation and analyses of figures. Like Rembrandt, he works in unflaring colors,

20

in golden browns and blacks with sudden illuminating spots of light that leave the backgrounds in shadowy mystery. The chioscuro of poetry is raised to a high plane by the writer. I have seen Robinson sitting in a darkening room with the last colors of the day on his face and the thought has come to me that Rembrandt would have rejoiced in painting the calm, rather weary features. It is the face of calm, distinguished patience; like the Flemish painter, he has known misunderstanding, neglect, and " the cold wash " of scorn. The personality of the man is the personality of his work. His is the sincerity of life-long convictions.

II.

The Tilbury figures made their appearance in Robinson's first book, and he has added to the gallery in practically every volume of his short pieces that has been issued since. Sometimes the town is not mentioned, but the idiosyncracies of these imaginary folk are recognizable in any setting. The poet has declared that Tilbury Town is no place in particular, but we may guess it is all places in general, Camelot as well as the Town Down the River. It is the mind of the poet. Into it venture the flotsam and jetsam of life, bedraggled figures, characters out-at-elbows (" unhappy night-birds " have always appealed to Robinson), " thwarted clerks and fiddlers " and majesty hiding a broken, troubled spirit. All of these people, sad, mad, feverish, posing, defeated, sum up for Robinson the total of life on this earth. They become, in a last analysis, a procession of figures, each carrying a cross. The poet stands slightly apart from them, viewing their futile gestures with a certain unperturbed gravity. An affectionate irony mingles with his sympathy at times.

22

This is existence as he sees it, and he will not prettify it even though the dark fabric of his work occasion the word " pessimist " in the mouths of unthinking readers. He knows what he is doing; he knows what he sees; he knows that in the final summing up " pessimist " is the last word that will be flung at him. Fatalistic he is, and he is fully cognizant of the unexpected blows of Destiny. Even the apparently successful personages, Richard Corey, " who glittered when he walked," and the man Flammonde, not a New Englander, but " from God knows where," cannot circumvent Destiny. They are in the grasp of unknown powers and make a brave show for a moment, only to be engulfed. Robinson makes no attempt to disguise the cruelty of life; that would be more cruel than life itself. He perceives it all, but he does not despair. In fortitude there is strength, and in living life fully and without cowardice there is satisfaction. These figures are the victims of human passions, of delusions. They are all victims, of fear, of envy, of life, of fame, of love. There is Flammonde, who can straighten out the lives of others, but not his own; John Evereldown, who is crazed about women; that extraordinary old loafer and philosopher, Captain Craig, who talks so engagingly about life, but cannot bend it to his purpose; Isaac and Archibald watching each other grow old and waiting eagerly for a sign of decay in the other; old Eben Flood lifting the jug to his lips, " like Roland's ghost winding an ancient horn," and toasting himself in the moonlight. Two men go into Shannon's and hear a tune, each coming away with his own memories alone. They are all ghosts, the phantasms of Robinson's speculations about life, the masks that he slips over his face and which are lighted by the grave glow of the spirit behind. They betray a sympathy for the submerged, a curiosity about defeated dreamers. Life's hardness is acknowledged, but it is faced with an almost oriental imperturbability. There is no suggestion of a bent knee or a bowing of the head. No least hint is to be discovered of the vociferous Henley spirit; Robinson is too sure of his convictions to shout loudly. His is the equanimity of one who understands transiences and eternal verities. In a sonnet to Monadnock Mountain he writes:

> And when the last of us, if we know how,
> See farther from ourselves than we do now,
> Assured with other sight than heretofore
> That we have done our mortal best and worst, —
> Your calm will be the same as when the first
> Assyrians went howling south to war.

It is a fatalistic peace, but it is the peace of one who has played

> In Art's long hazard, where no man may choose
> Whether he play to win or toil to lose.

Behind that fatalistic peace is the hope, a far one but one that is assuredly real, that is summed up in " The Man Against the Sky." Here is the crystallization of Robinson's philosophy, the unadorned discernment of that golden thread that glimmers through all his work. His Tilbury figures, helpless as they are, at least have this consolation shining like a far beacon before them. It is a cold faith, perhaps, but it possesses the iciness of logic. It is based upon that " common creed of common-sense " that Robinson reiterated in his earliest poems. With the consistency of the philosopher who hugs to his heart a system of things, the poet has developed and deepened his idea of the scheme of existence. His " Man Against the Sky " is all men.

> Whatever the dark road he may have taken,
> This man who stood on high
> And faced alone the sky,
> Whatever drove or lured or guided him, —
> A vision answering a faith unshaken,
> An easy trust assumed of easy trials, ___
> A sick negation born of weak denials,
> A crazed abhorrence of an old condition,

25

A blind attendance on a brief ambition, —
Whatever stayed him or derided him,
His way was even as ours;
And we, with all our wounds and all our powers,
Must each wait alone at his own height
Another darkness or another light.

The stern questioning note which ends " The Man Against the Sky " has been misread by certain people, who have taken the conclusion without the profound " if " that is implicit in it and from it drawn the conviction that Robinson is a complete materialist. How far this is from the truth a careful reading of the poem will show. If we are no more than we seem to be, he asserts, if we are " no greater than the noise we make along one blind atomic pilgrimage," then it were better to die. But the poet does not think so. He is not so sure of this dark, material snuffing-out of all things. It is impossible to conceive that the whole of our colored, majestical, strange and exalted existence can be so ordered. There is " an orient Word that will not be erased," something that comes " in incommunicable gleams too permanent for dreams." Commonsense should convince us that this faith must have a divine source in some mysterious place. Science cannot tell us

Why man should hunger through another season
To find out why " 'twere better late than soon
To go away."

" Shall we," he gravely propounds,

" .   .   .   because Eternity records
Too vast an answer for the time-worn words
We spell, whereof so many are dead that once
In our capricious lexicons
Were so alive and final, hear no more
The Word itself.   .   .   ."

This is, perhaps, a negative faith, but it is as
essentially a faith as any other.   It is a calm, dispassionate attempt at reasoning, an effort to be
entirely impartial and permit the natural instincts to
arrive at conclusions through the cold application
of commonsense and logic toward a great question
that has been too often lost in the excitement of
mad emotionalism.

With such an attitude in mind we can better
understand the Tilbury Town figures and the angle
from which they are approached by the poet.   Although his characters may despair themselves, we
may rest assured that their creator does not despair
equally with them.   All of them will come into their
heritage.   Flammonde will reach that high still
place where he may put his own life in order as
beautifully as he has fashioned the lives of others.

Captain Craig, who cried " Trombones! " before he died, will turn the corner of Time and find his philosophical disquisitions all plain before him. The two nameless men who heard the nameless song in Shannon's indubitably bear on their way toward the source of the emotion in that song.

III

It was Robinson's inexhaustible interest in the specific spirits of men that drew him to such historical personages as Shakespeare, John Brown, Lincoln, Aaron Burr, Alexander Hamilton, Napoleon and Rembrandt. In every portrait the individuality is the clothing of eternal and universal traits. John Brown is an aspect of the fanatic of all time just as Rembrandt is the neglected and misunderstood genius of all time. It was a more general absorption of the soul that took the poet to St. Paul and Lazarus. Here he was picturing more than humanity; he was holding up the great Life-Stream and approaching the hidden mystery. From his meditation on life and the universality of traits sprang his Merlin, Vivien, Lancelot and Guenevere. They are intensely individual, and yet they are symbols moving in frame-works fashioned after the shifting and unstabilized structures of our modern days. Robinson's most recent endeavors have been in putting individualities in contact so that the clashes become high expressions of the maladies of the soul and the perplexed hearts of men. The succession of themes, certainly unconscious on Robinson's part, is yet illuminating. First, the creation of single imaginary figures; then the revitalizing of historical personages from the data and atmospheres they have left behind them; then the original representation of legendary figures who stand for certain spiritual manifestations, their re-application, as it were, to our modern times; and, finally, the creation of groups of imaginary figures in juxtaposition, acting out life. From the very first the dramatic instinct has been strong in Robinson; together with the analytic study of character goes the drama of personalities in contact. And from the very first, accompanying these major efforts, are the sonnets and lyrics, subsidiary but important expressions of Robinson's thought. They are the foot-notes to life and we must not be surprised if more often than not we find packed in these notes the cerebral substance of the major achievements.

In turning to the historical figures we are met immediately by Shakespeare. " Ben Jonson Entertains a Man From Stratford " is a poem in which the art of Robinson may be studied at its finest blooming. This human being, Shakespeare, torn between immortal dreams and his desire for the House of Stratford, lives and breathes as he is outlined through the gruff kindliness of Ben Jonson's monologue. He is a mortal man, somewhat a fatalist, who can ruminate about life in this fashion:

"Your fly will serve as well as anybody,
And what's his hour? He flies, and flies, and flies,
And in his fly's mind has a brave appearance;
And then your spider gets him in her net,
And eats him out and hangs him up to dry,
That's Nature, the kind mother of us all.
And then your slattern house-maid swings her broom,
And where's your spider? And that's Nature, also.
It's Nature, and it's Nothing. It's all Nothing.
It's all a world where bugs and emperors
Go singularly back to the same dust,
Each in his time; and the old, ordered stars
That sang together, Ben, will sing the same
Old stave tomorrow."

Yet in spite of this vein Ben Jonson declares of him:

Today the clouds are with him, but anon
He'll out of 'em enough to shake the tree
Of life itself and bring down fruit unheard-of, —
And, throwing in the bruised and whole together,
Prepare a wine to make us drunk with wonder;
And if he live, there'll be a sunset spell
Thrown over him as over a glassed lake
That yesterday was all a black wild water.

Surely no better portrait has ever been painted of "this mad, careful, proud, indifferent Shakespeare."

Then there is "The Three Taverns," that remarkable effort in which St. Paul reveals himself. It purports to be a speech of Paul's to Christian

31

friends who come out from Rome as far as the place called The Three Taverns to welcome the militant apostle. Besides showing an assiduous study of extant writings of and references to Paul, the poem exhibits an authentic and lofty utterance that sets it somewhat apart from the other portraits. This tolerant Paul, who preaches that the Kingdom is within one and who bids his listeners

> Make, then, for all your fears a place to sleep
> With all your faded sins; nor think yourselves
> Egregrious and alone for your defects
> Of youth and yesterday,

looms before the reader as a living figure. The character of Paul is tantalizing. It has been stated that shortly before his death William Vaughan Moody was contemplating a poetic play upon this one Biblical personage who seems so close to our contemporary life. Paul was indubitably a man. He was a courageous, gruff, valiant, exalted figure, a militant Christian. Robinson makes of him a man advanced in years, somewhat of a seer, a prophet who can say:

> The world is here
> To-day, and it may not be gone to-morrow;
> For there are millions, and there may be more,
> To make in turn a various estimation

Of its old ills and ashes, and the traps
Of its apparent wrath. Many with ears
That hear not shall have ears given to them,
And then they shall hear strangely. Many with eyes
That are incredulous of the Mystery
Shall yet be driven to feel, and then to read
Where language has an end and is a veil,
Not woven of our words. Many that hate
Their kind are soon to know that without love
Their faith is but the perjured name of nothing.
I that have done some hating in my time
See now no time for hate; I that have left,
Fading behind me like familiar lights
That are to shine no more for my returning,
Home, friends and honors — I that have lost all else
For wisdom, and the wealth of it, say now
To you that out of wisdom has come love,
That measures and is of itself the measure
Of works and hope and faith.

The poem on John Brown is another piece of exalted tone. It is not so successful as " The Three Taverns," principally because it is not so ambitious as that effort, but it does bring home many truths that sixty years have not dimmed. John Brown's last words in his speech to his wife are:

I shall have more to say when I am dead.

Here is another militant prophet. There is even prophecy in " On the Way." One begins to see that the historical figures who interest Robinson the most are the valiant builders, the men who sacrifice all for the sake of futurity. It is the world about us that must be made better. It is the beams in our own eyes that must be plucked out if Time is to greet a race that walks more sturdily in the sunlight than we do today. Existence is against us; we are against ourselves, for we are but mortal and compact with mortal failings. Yet it is from ourselves that we must gather sufficient strength to front the ages. Children of darkness in search of the light are we, and we may gather from Robinson that more often than not it is ourselves who hide that light, our own shadows that fall across it and dim it.

IV

When Robinson turned to the Arthurian legends
there was a sceptical outcry. The idea that these
themes had been embalmed for all time in Tenny-
sonian treacle persisted and many readers failed to
see that Robinson had an intensely modern purpose.
Those readers should go back and read these poems
again. " Merlin " contains a picture of a falling
world, of an old order breaking down and giving
place to a new; and this was just what Robinson
saw in contemporary life about him. There is a
symbolism in " Merlin " that should be plain by
now. " Lancelot " is more of a story and may be
read as such, although it, too, contains a certain
symbolic significance. In reading through these
poems again it is astonishing how " Merlin " stands
out as a work of beauty. Its pages are starred with
such passages as this:

He bowed his head
And kissed the ten small fingers he was holding,
As calmly as if each had been a son;
Although his heart was leaping and his eyes
Had sight for nothing save a swimming crimson
Between two glimmering arms. " More like a flower

Tonight," he said, as now he scanned again
The immemorial meaning of her face
And drew it nearer to his eyes. It seemed
A flower of wonder with a crimson stem
Came leaning slowly and regretfully.
To meet his will — a flower of change and peril
That had a clinging blossom of warm olive
Half stifled with a tyranny of black,
And held the wayward fragrance of a rose
Made woman by delirious alchemy.
She raised her face and yoked his willing neck
With half her weight; and with hot lips that left
The world with only one philosophy
For Merlin or for Anaxagoras,
Called his to meet them and in one long hush
Of capture to surrender and make hers
The last of anything that might remain
Of what was now their beardless wizardry.
Then slowly she began to push herself
Away, and slowly Merlin let her go
As far from him as his outstretching hands
Could hold her fingers while his eyes ·had all
The beauty of the woodland and the world
Before him in the firelight, like a nymph
Of cities, or a queen a little weary
Of inland stillness and immortal trees.

The tonal color of " Merlin " is crimson and
green; that of " Lancelot " is white and gold. In
both poems we have evidence of that bewilderingly
sudden capture of beauty in single lines, a virtue of
Robinson's poetry that has never been sufficiently
emphasized. Lines like that one describing Lance-

lot's thought of Guenevere, like a star " too far to reach but too fair not to follow," need no praise. The achievement is self-evident.

There can be but small doubt but that these Arthurian poems will eventually rank high in the annals of American poetry, but it may be some time before readers adjust themselves to the manner of these efforts and properly disentangle them from the taint of Tennyson. There is no Tennyson in " Merlin " and " Lancelot." Tennyson, if it were possible for him to read these poems, would be bewildered, rather shocked, and wholly helpless before their cerebral intensity.

V

Robinson's last two books, if we except the " Collected Poems," have been narratives where the interest centered upon the situation and juxtaposition of figures as well as the characterization. "Avon's Harvest " is a dramatic study of hatred permeated with an eery sense of the supernatural, and " Roman Bartholow " is a magnificent handling of the triangle in a new and intensely cerebral fashion. This last-mentioned poem will undoubtedly occasion disquietude in those casual and superficial readers of Robinson's work who are more concerned with their own predilections than with an organized understanding of natural poetical growth. It is the fashion with these Solons to affirm that Robinson's work grows more intricate and obscure in each volume. The main reason for this statement is the ʄact that their brains do not keep pace with the poet. In one maladorous medley of misconceptions which was occasioned by the publication of " Roman Bartholow " the writer attempted to show that Robinson's work had declined steadily since his first volume. Any comparison of " The Children of the Night " with the richness and vast maturity of

"The Man Against the Sky" speedily will show how absurd any such statement is. A great poet must express himself infinitely because there is infinite matter in him. His output must present various forms. It is monstrous to expect that he will repeat his successes *ad infinitum*. He must go on to new endeavors. Incidentally, it is amusing to note that among those young critics who exclaim at the "obscurity" of Robinson are several who are valiant defenders of T. S. Eliot's "The Waste Land."

Robinson will go on in the pathway which he has chosen for himself without any consideration of his critics. His procession of masks will picture life as the poet conceives it to be. Because he stands alone, and because he *can* stand alone, he takes his place as America's great contribution to modern letters since Walt Whitman. His work answers the question, What has been Robinson's idea? I should say: He tried to map the labyrinth of the heart. And, after years of writing and meditation, his conclusion, fatalistic enough, is

> That earth has not a school where we may go
> For wisdom, or for more than we may know.

EMILY DICKINSON

EMILY DICKINSON

IN the poetry of Emily Dickinson we over-
hear the solitary ejaculations of a personality whose last thought was an audience.
It is as though the wind had blown open a
long-locked door and, standing upon the
threshold, we gaze into a quiet chamber where the
occupant, wholly unaware of our inquiring eyes and
ears, goes about her daily affairs entirely unadorned
for the pleasure or profit of any chance visitors.
This is entirely delightful and mentally invigorating.
The revelations and betrayals are so spontaneous,
so much the result of sudden urges and artless
moods. There is no considered singing here, no
careful compilations of thoughts or moods, no curi-
ously carved and finished stanzas. The poet is
entirely ignorant of a possible audience, so much so
that her verses come to us as the artless, broken
melodies of the thrush. The thought is often in-
complete, the rhythm becomes uncertain at times;
many of the short pieces seem like fragments, jot-
tings and comments upon the border of life.

As Emily Dickinson was a recluse in life, so is her
poetry the unpremeditated foot-notes to her solitary

43

existence. Her poems are recluses, rather unconscious of the polished garb that clothes that
more self-contained inspiration which walks boldly
through the market-place. Her concern was not
with matters of technique, stanza-forms, meters,
logical successions of thought; it was mainly to set
down the chance moment that had flamed with a
more than ordinary flash before her calm, meditative
mind. The result is a series of strange jewels, glittering stones set upon the unobtrusive thread of her
days. If we are to immediately note the prime virtue which sets Emily Dickinson's work apart from
the transcendental wave that engulfed the New
England of her time, we must deliberately accept
that uncouthness of technique which occasionally
becomes, in a last analysis, an admirable adjunct in
the piercing suddenness of her revelations and concern ourselves only with the phraseology, the sharp
and biting arrangements of words that reveal the
poet as one of those few and astonishing personages
who can circumscribe so much beyond the power of
mere syllables. There is a natural magic here that
is inborn. No practice can make possible the best
stanzas by Emily Dickinson. They are the flashes
struck into existence by the contact of an extraordinary mind with life, and especially nature.

Three aspects of Emily Dickinson's art stand out, aspects that make her essentially herself, and if we consider these in order perhaps it is possible to convey some idea of her magic in a short article. These are: (1) the extraordinary power of exact description of nature, a power that compresses an entire paragraph into a phrase; (2) the concentration of meaning, which follows naturally upon the first aspect; and (3) the abrupt application of adjectives and verbs, which, of course, is a natural corollary of the first two aspects. These three aspects merge into one another and become, in any summing up, what we denominate as the poetical style of Emily Dickinson. How they were attained is a mystery. She was born at Amherst, Massachusetts, on December 10, 1830, and died there, aged fifty-five, on May 13, 1886. Excepting for the yearly reception tendered by her father, who was treasurer of Amherst College, she lived the existence of a hermit, writing her poems for her few friends, among whom may be noted Thomas Wentworth Higginson. This extraordinary method of life might be calculated to develop a self-consciousness in her, a pretty awkwardness, as it were, yet it seems to have done nothing of the kind. Report has it that she acted the perfect hostess at the yearly reception, conducting herself with a simple dignity and self-assurance that might be expected in a more cosmopolitan person. The absence of literary advice and companionship may be suspected to have both aided and injured her art. It aided it in that it made it possible for her to be wholly herself, to follow no influences, to let no self-consciousness detract from the admirable assurance of her poise. She was not concerned with doubts and misgivings as to her art, for she did not weigh it in comparison with the contemporary work of intellectual New England. Complete absence of influences and competitive values made Emily Dickinson herself. On the other hand, this lack of literary companionship and conversation possibly tended to leave uncorrected the crudities, gaucheries, and frequent stumbling of her stanzaic forms. She could but refine upon herself and there was no one to illustrate by quick wit and example the *culs-de-sac* into which she often blundered. It has been asserted that these awkwardnesses of stanzaic form aided her work, made vivid the thought contained in the poem, and while this, luckily enough, is sometimes the case, it cannot be accepted as a complete truth. No one but the most emphatic of Emily Dickinson's disciples would assert that there are not times when the uncouthness of structure and phraseology injured her conception. The abruptnesses do come at intervals with the fresh, naive magic of sudden revelations, but not with consistent regularity. Indeed, they completely destroy some of the poems, and one can but long for that carefully combed, selected, and edited volume of Emily Dickinson's works that will do more to establish her as the finest American woman-poet that we have ever possessed than the volumes now available.

In turning to the consideration of her beautiful capacity for describing nature, perhaps the strongest of her virtues, we might as well march into the woodland to the strain of the last three verses of her " Summer's Armies ":

> The dreamy butterflies bestir,
> Lethargic pools resume the whir
> Of last year's sundered tune.
> From some old fortress on the sun
> Baronial bees march, one by one,
> In murmuring platoon!
>
> The robins stand as thick today
> As flakes of snow stood yesterday,
> On fence and roof and twig.
> The orchis binds her feather on
> For her old lover, Don the Sun,
> Revisiting the bog!

Without commander, countless, still,
The regiment of wood and hill
In bright detachment stand .
Behold! What multitudes are these?
The children of whose turbaned seas,
Or what Circassian land?

" The regiment of wood and hill " was known,
every individual, to Emily Dickinson. Birds, flowers, grass, trees, mushrooms, sunset and sunrise,
wind and rain and snow, darkness and light, all of
these things came to her prescient with rich magic.
Before her eyes the little things loomed with an
actual majesty, and much of her imagery is concerned with these revelations of the greatness implicit in minute aspects of nature. There was a
Blake-like touch in her; assuredly she could see " a
world in a grain of sand " and " hold infinity in the
palm of the hand." All of these things were rare
ministrants to her spirit. They reacted upon her,
and she responded with the sensitivity of an Æolian
harp.

The red upon the hill
Taketh away my will.

She lived and died with the seasons, for they were
individualities to her. The mountain sat " in his
eternal chair." He was the " grandfather of the
days," the ancestor of dawn. The setting sun was

" little yellow boys and girls " climbing a purple
stile,

> Till when they reached the other side,
> A dominie in grey
> Put gently up the evening bars,
> And led the flock away.

The butterfly emerges " like a lady from a door,"
and " her pretty parasol " is seen contracting over
the hay-fields. The oriole is " the Jesuit of the
orchards " and the wind is all sorts of persons.
Even the tiny stone has an individuality of its own,
for she sings:

> How happy is the little stone
> That rambles in the road alone.
> And doesn't care about careers,
> And exigencies never fears;
> Whose coat of elmental brown
> A passing universe put on;
> And independent as the sun,
> Associates or glow alone,
> Fulfilling absolute decree
> In casual simplicity.

Indeed, with such a world of personalities about
her how is it possible to call Emily Dickinson a hermit? She had her own world; it was streaming with
friends and confidantes. Everywhere she turned she
met the face or the aspect of one of her familiars.
This enchanted largesse of nature is perfectly re-

49

vealed to us through that second admirable aspect
of Emily Dickinson's art,— the power of concen-
trating meaning in short lines. She can write

> As imperceptibly as grief
> The summer lapsed away,

and, while it seems simple, it is not. One word,
"lapsed," makes the whole difference. But to note
Emily Dickinson's high power of concentration we
must turn to those immortal eight lines which alone
would have given the poet the right to be considered
among the finest writers in America:

> My life closed twice before its close;
>   It yet remains to see
> If Immortality unveil
>   A third event to me.
>
> So huge, so hopeless to conceive,
>   As these that twice befell.
> Parting is all we know of heaven,
>   And all we need of hell.

What can be said about these lines? They may be
quoted, and after that we must be silent. And
again, what strange nuances are implied in these
lines?

> I've seen a dying eye
> Run round and round a room
> In search of something, as it seemed,

50

> Then cloudier become;
> And then, obscure with fog,
> And then be soldered down,
> Without disclosing what it be,
> 'T were blessed to have seen.

These quotations are the concentrated heart of poetry. With the simplest words and with a rare art that is essentially artless she secured effects that many a more finished and over-theorized poet would have fumbled badly. Part of this beauty is implicit in that third aspect of the poet's work,— the abrupt application of words which become unexpected revelations as she places them.

There is something extremely modern here, and it is astonishing to note how much Emily Dickinson anticipated certain genres of our own contemporary poetry. She possessed the precise eye that is so demanded by the imagists; she was never addicted to over-elaborate trimmings; she never (or, at least, rarely) dropped into cliches or time-tarnished poetical phraseology. Most of all, she was essentially vital and always herself. Her philosophy, of course, is mainly transcendental in its larger aspects, but together with it ran a rare pantheism. Writing of love or death, her very simplicity gave an added poignancy to the theme. How much she actually suffered is her own secret, but we may guess that

51

there were certain crises in her like that shook her terribly. The death of her sister was one of them. At times there is almost an Elizabethan starkness in her lines, a dry hardness that suggests the less extravagant stanzas of Dr. John Donne. The similarity is extremely vague, for Donne and Emily Dickinson possess no actual points of contact. It is rather in the abrupt twist of the phrase, in lines like

> What if I say I shall not wait?
> What if I burst the fleshly gate
> And pass, escaped, to thee?
> What if I file this mortal off,
> See where it hurt me, — that's enough, —
> And wade in liberty?

" What if I file this mortal off " is a fair example of the use of an unexpected word. It is a conceit, of course, but a sombre conceit. Indeed, in the poems concerned with death we find more often than not a sombre note. Emily Dickinson felt the weight of grief, although her ethical environment undoubtedly removed her from the danger of despair. At times the thought of death fascinated her, and more than once she pictured that state between sleeping and waking when the being is at pause. Sometimes the feeling came suddenly in broad daylight, as in this poem:

It was not death, for I stood up,
And all the dead lie down;
It was not night, for all the bells
Put out their tongues, for noon.

It was not frost, for on my flesh
I felt siroccos crawl, —
Nor fire, for just my marble feet
Could keep a chancel cool.

And yet it tasted like them all;
The figures I have seen
Set orderly, for burial,
Reminded me of mine,

As if my life were shaven
And fitted to a frame,
And could not breathe without a key;
And 'twas like midnight, some.

When everything that ticked has stopped,
And space stares, all around,
Or grisly frosts, first autumn morns,
Repeal the beating ground.

But most like chaos, — stopless, cool, —
Without a chance or spar,
Or even a report of land
To justify despair.

Certain elements of this poem bring us to the real heart of Emily Dickinson's poetry. She was a mystic. She turned the eyes of her spirit inward and led an intense life that was unalloyed by distractions.

Colored by the rare, lonely, answering flowering of nature about her, she meditated on Time and Eternity, on the vague mystery of Love, on the " easy nonchalance " of Death. It was better so that she led the secluded life which was to be her portion in a world where she possessed nothing particularly in common with the human beings about her. She was the rarest emanation of the old New England life, the brooding mystic who is yet lightened by the brief gaiety of rich summers and barbaric autumns. Time cannot but gather to her name as the years march by for the place which she secured for herself in the annals of American poesy is one which must remain unchallenged forever. The conditions which made her, the philosophical atmosphere in which she came to maturity, have vanished. Her flowering was unusual, but one which might have been expected. She has become part of a great heritage.

" THE INCOMPARABLE MAX "

"THE INCOMPARABLE MAX"

I

MAX, I am told, is a little man with outrageously long eye-lashes. He lives in a villa in Rapallo, very near Gordon Craig, and when the ambitious visitor rings his doorbell he pops his head out of a sort of cupola and studies the unsuspecting form beneath him. Just what requisites are necessary to gain admittance to the villa have never been satisfactorily explained. Perhaps the hat (the top of the hat) has something to do with it. Certainly the bird's-eye view which Max obtains of his prospective callers can hardly convey the intellectual calibre of the knocker at the gate. However, rumor has it that people *do* get in if they wait long enough (I am told he is quite leisurely in answering the bell), and when they do they are face to face with the unparalleled master of the modern English essay.

It is probably quite nerve-racking to be an entire movement in one's self — that is, if one ever stops to painfully cogitate about it. But Max can hardly be accused of self-consciousness. He is too well-bred for that. Well-bred individuals are never self-conscious, although they may sometimes suffer from the self-consciousness of others. Self-consciousness is indubitably a feeling of inferiority. Max never experienced this feeling. One cannot slyly smile at one's contemporaries all one's life and feel inferior. And this is what Max has done. His parodies and caricatures form an unmistakable criticism of the literary, art, and political life through which he has airily passed, flower in button-hole and silk hat neatly tilted above those historic eye-lashes. I must insist on the boutonniere and silk hat. The art of Max absolutely requires them, and if, through some sad negligence he has never acquired them, he should proceed instantly to the nearest flower-stand and haberdasher in Rapallo and repair the inexplicable lack. It is as easy to imagine Whistler without an eye-glass as Max Beerbohm without a silk-hat and boutonniere.

Harold Williams, in his amiable, well-documented "Modern English Writers," declared anent Max: "His true fame will rest upon his genius as a draughtsman and caricaturist." I must boggle a bit at this, for, rising from the re-perusal of half a dozen volumes of Max's prose, I find myself positively enchanted. Every true essay is an adventure; it does not matter what it is about providing it relates an adventure. It may be any sort of an adventure, material, spiritual, discursive, humorous. It may be about servant girls or trained seals, riding in a train or taking a bath. It may even be about Spring! But there must be a twist in the writer's mind, a twist that is conveyed to the reader, in short — an adventure. Adventures (at least in the essay form) are not necessarily unexpected. They may be but a sudden re-acquaintance, a delightful remembrance. Having mentioned Spring as a theme for the essayist, let me return to it for an illustration. Everybody who writes touches on Spring sooner or later. One might just as well hope to be a woman who walks down Fifth Avenue without looking into a single shop window as a writer who does not pause to regard Spring. Now there are endless essays, poems, and paragraphs concocted about Spring. Most of them are bad, vapid reiterations which merely serve to show that one's heart is in the right place, anyway. But occasionally the reader puts down a Spring essay or poem with a new realization of what the season means, a clutch at the heart, a giddy feeling in the head that means disaster and delay to ordinary tasks, a warm tolerance toward the whole world. This is because the author circumscribed an adventure. His individuality illumined the old subject in a new way. There was a twist in his mind. He viewed Spring from a new angle, or he emphasized its meaning with a high degree of personality. This is what Max Beerbohm does to the essay form. He makes adventures of his essays. His prankish personality relumes the ancient lamps. Servants or cosmetics or statues or Algernon Swinburne or the Yellow Nineties, seen through his eyes and portrayed by his debonair (there is no other word for it) pen, are not the servants or cosmetics or statues or Algernon Swinburne or Yellow Nineties with which we have been acquainted heretofore. At the same time, we do not doubt but what they are authentic servants, etc.

I have mentioned the Yellow Nineties. That decade witnessed the growth of Max to maturity. The influences that permeated English letters during that period have long ceased to exist, and nothing remains but some palely delicate poetry, some plays, the green carnation, and Max Beerbohm. It is difficult to classify Max, to associate him with the

Nineties, with Wilde or Symons or Dowson or
Beardsley. He asserted once that he belonged to
the Beardsley period, but his tongue must have been
in his cheek. He did not mean that he was a disciple
of the lean and spidery Aubrey; he meant that he
passed simultaneously with the short life of that
great draughtsman. It was merely an example of
Max's *blague*. Like the men of the nineties, he was
a trifler in the courts of Beauty, but he wore his rue
with a difference. Where the others wept, he
laughed. When they crept into the arms of the
Roman Catholic Church for spiritual comfort, he
went to the theatre. He did not take his artificiality with the seriousness of those others, those others
who remain immortalized in his sketch of Enoch
Soames. Max is delicate, impersonal, a maker of
dainty grimaces at seriousness. Yet he can establish his undertones of seriousness when he so desires
in the most poignant fashion. Who can read his
description of Swinburne in "And Even Now " without catching frequent flashes of the undeniable love
he bore the great master of song and without taking
away a vivid realization of the last days of the
tenant of The Pines, Putney? And Enoch Soames,
who has been mentioned above, is drawn with tears
close behind the laughter. He represents more than

a humorous figure to Max, for he stands for the youth of the essayist. In such a milieu did he come to full maturity. Enoch is redolent of " fin-de-siecle " days. The London cafes of twenty-five years ago knew his footsteps intimately; his lugubrious face was a familiar spectacle on the boulevards of Paris. He is exaggerated, of course, but it would be difficult to point out where exaggeration ends and reality begins so closely are they knit.

Someone has affirmed that Max's caricatures are essays and his essays are caricatures. This is probably true. Of course, there is a delightful enlargement of the truth in the delicate prose of Max. That is part of his charm and an integral part of his style. He must enlarge to impress, and the result is a figure that grows remarkably lifelike and yet too whimsically delightful to be quite human. They are extraordinary human beings even in their lesser moments, from Zuleika Dobson and her Oxford boys to the Happy Hypocrite and the astounding gallery of the " Seven Men." Max is more than a humorist — he is an ironist, almost a happy Voltaire, at times. His irony is exquisite in its nuances, a carefully-wrought workmanship that grows almost *precieuse* at times. But so charming, so diverting and so airy is this approach to preciousness that it

62

wards off petulance.   Max never laughs outright.
That would be a little vulgar.   He provokes one
with a sudden darting smile, sometimes with a half-
concealed chuckle that becomes memorable in its
implications the more one ponders about it.

II

It is difficult to take Max seriously because he has never taken himself seriously. It was in 1896 that he gravely collected the half-dozen essays he had contributed to various periodicals, including The Yellow Book, in a slim, red-covered volume and published them as " The Works of Max Beerbohm." The ironic seriousness of his valedictory to that book will never be forgotten by those who read it. It is still funny, although the lapse of years has dimmed some of the effrontery of the gesture. He declared himself outmoded, a creature of the Beardsley school. " I shall write no more," he declared, and settled back with an outrageously comical gesture to bask in the fame which he complacently claimed as his portion. The attitude was beautiful, although it was a little conscious, not conscious enough, I haste to add, to be self-conscious. We may judge that the attitude was more of a laugh at his contemporaries than anything else. They were *so* utterly serious! They were like the gentleman in W. E. Henley's forgotten ballad:

> I'm on for any Art that's 'Igh;
> I talks as quick as I can splutter;
> I keeps a Dado on the sly;
> In short, my form's the Bloomin' Utter!

It was the habit to be intense during the early Nineties, to go the limit, to take one's self with astounding seriousness. It was an era of attitudes, a decade of deliberate disguises. Men wore their masks boldly and the procession generally moved to the delicate music of Verlaine. *Fin de siecle* was the battle-cry and decadence was the more or less conscious objective. Victorianism was dead; its last trumpet had sounded when the Laureate's body passed into the Abbey; and although such major artists as Swinburne, Meredith and Hardy still survived, they had long proved their dissimilarity from those men of letters whom we term Victorians. And the feeling that an era was dead must have been emphasized by the literal fact that it was the fag-end of a century. For no other reason could the phrase " fin-de-siecle " have attained the prominence which it did.

Into this era of green carnations, Yellow Books, and pallid, passionate verses stepped Max, " the incomparable Max," as George Bernard Shaw dubbed him in *The Saturday Review*. He brought what Holbrook Jackson neatly terms urbanity. His self-possession was delightfully impudent, an impudence that is broader in his caricatures than in his essays. His delectable " Diminuendo " to the

" Works " fooled no one. It was but to be expected that within a few years he should publish " More " and " The Happy Hypocrite." He has continued to carry the foolery of the title of his first book through his entire list of published volumes of essays. After " More " came " Yet Again," and but a year ago appeared "And Even Now." Though the Yellow Nineties had their saffron days, wielded their influences on English letters and settled back into a comfortable niche ransacked only by literary historians and young men between the ages of seventeen and twenty-one, Max has gone merrily on. His style has mellowed to some degree; it is profounder (especially in such things as the essays in " Seven Men "); but he is unmistakably the same writer who contributed to the first issue of Henry Harland's Yellow Book the famed " Defense of Cosmetics." This essay, together with Arthur Symon's " Defence of Patchouli," may be taken as a credo of the Nineties. The only difference between the two efforts is that Mr. Symons undoubtedly meant what he said, while Max didn't mean a word of it. Who remembers that first essay by Max? It was compact with such prose as this:

"Was it not at Capua that they had a whole street where nothing was sold but dyes and unguents? We must have such a street, and, to fill our new Seplosia, our

66

Arcade of Unguents, all herbs and minerals and live creatures shall give of their substance. The white cliffs of
Albion shall be ground to powder for Loveliness, and
perfumed by the ghost of many a little violet. The fluffy
eider-ducks, that are swimming around the pond, shall
lose their feathers, that the powder-puff may be moonlight as it passes over Loveliness' lovely face."

This is laughable, of course, but so charmingly,
so beautifully laughable. Like many of Max's essays, there is evident a deliberate playing with
words and images and thoughts, a gentle juggling
with feathery conceits in the rosy air. There are
frequent moments when the essayist grows almost
euphuistic. The ghost of John Lyly pirouettes behind the sentences, but the pirouettes of Max himself
are more spontaneous. No labored play with extravagant images is to be found in the " Works,"
" More," " Yet Again " or "And Even Now." In
" Euphues " the modern reader hears the clicking of
the author's brain; the artificiality is so great that it
smashes like an eggshell when struck by a gust of
thought. This is far from the case with Max. Behind his images and quaint turns of phraseology is
the supple silver skeleton of agile thought. The
satirist is there; so, too, is the ironist; and always
apparent is the dancing flash of lifted wit. Of
course, there was always something artificial in the

Nineties, a prettiness that surfeited the reader at times, a Herrick blown hollow. Max must have known this from the beginning. His slyness of perception kept his tongue in his cheek during the era of " slim gilt boys " and " morbidezzas."

And always he has remained urbane, a creature of the town, viewing his little conscious world with a wise and gently satiric eye. An aristocratic finish glitters over his essays like an aura. Max is nothing if not the perfect gentleman. He is as carefully finished as an English box-hedge. One instinctively beholds him in Hyde Park, carrying his stick with distinction. Above all things, he belongs to the city. Even when he writes of the country (and he can do this in the most ingratiating manner) he suggests the more select purlieus of London. T. S. Eliot's Prufrock bewailed the fact that he had measured out his life with coffee spoons, but it is to be suspected that such a procedure would carry its degree of self-congratulation and satisfaction on the part of Max Beerbohm. Perhaps, on second thought, Max would prefer tea spoons. His laughter, in the words of one of the New Poets, " tinkles among the teacups." He balances his cake with assurance, and hails a cab with a flourish as carefully studied as Napoleon's gesture before the Pyramids. " Soldiers," cried the Emperor, " forty centuries are gazing down upon you!" "Ah," cries Max, nimbly hopping into a cab, " Forty Duchesses are gazing up at you!" And yet he is not self-conscious! He was born to it; it is an integral part of his nature. Perhaps he doesn't ride in cabs or drink tea or carry a stick in the actuality; but the spiritual Max, the Max who rises from the fragrant pages of the essays, does. It would be an entertaining (albeit quite hopeless) procedure to some day recreate a number of authors from the pages of their books, fashioning them into the likenesses that their work suggests them to be, and Max, I feel sure, would be the Dandy of them all.

His urbanity is undisputed, and yet there is a sweetness of sympathy (particularly in his later work) that runs far beneath the surface. The imaginary figures that make up " Seven Men," for instance, arouse our cordial liking even while we laugh at them. The merriment is tempered by an art that walks definitively on the high plane of authentic literature. Who can fail to pity poor Enoch Soames, the much be-caped poet of fin-de-siecle days, who desired so much to be re-born 2,000 years hence that he might see what Fame had done to him, and who *is* born again and who discovers that his only

69

claim to immortality is this very article which Max
Beerbohm is writing about him? Even Savonarola
Brown, he of the bulging brow and the astounding
tragedy, grows loveable while we laugh at him.
Perhaps part of this sweetness of sympathy springs
from memory. It is possible that these exaggerated
characters are the crystallized presentations of
movements at which Max has laughed gleefully in
times past. There is nothing that arouses our sympathy so much as the things and persons who awak-
ened our humor "in the brave days when we were
twenty-one." We love them for the delight they
brought us, and we know that the memory of our
laughter would not have stayed with us had there
not been something of more than momentary value
in the occasions of our amusement. Max has gone
through life laughing, or, rather, gently smiling, and
he has now reached the age where a certain sentimentality makes its inevitable entrance. With the
passage of years and the growth of a sound spiritual
equanimity comes an abiding tolerance and kindliness of vision. The edges of those bright weapons
of irony, used so skillfully in times of old, are soft-
ened. The wit of Max, so like a rapier and at its
rarest development in the caricatures, still flashes in
the sunlight, but it does not pierce too deeply. In-

70

deed, it is to be doubted if Max ever intended to pierce anyone or anything fiercely. He views life with a beaming eye, a little maliciously at times, but most of the while with a satiric twinkle. If illusions creep upon him and he looks back with a smile that is a little sad, we must understand that he came to maturity in a period that is now nothing but illusions. No man could live through the 1890's and not, sooner or later, fall victim to the legendary spell that makes those days more real today than they were when they actually existed. " Daisy Bell " was not more melodious than " The Love Nest," but it can arouse memories that the later song will never evoke. Lottie Collins was not more talented than her daughter, Jose, yet Lottie's scarlet skirt will serve as an oriflamme into the battlefields of memory for many a sedate banker of today. And so Max Beerbohm, born in 1872, must poetize a bit about the men he knew when Aubrey Beardsley was the rage and Leonard Smithers knew what good books were.

A REVENANT OF THE NINETIES

A REVENANT OF THE NINETIES

AUGUSTUS JOHN has painted a portrait of Arthur Symons. It is the face of an old man, bearded and seamed, the bony forehead bulging above the tired, calm eyes. Here is a map upon which is drawn the progress of time, the march of those inevitable, fluctuating moods that shake the sophisticated lover of material things. Here are the eyes that have quested so strenuously for a visible beauty, a beauty of flowers, faces, rings, dancers, cities, all of the intolerable transiences that so insistently remind us that Time travels like a cruel river washing along in its swiftly-moving waters every desire of the heart. Here is the mouth grown strangely hungry and regretful. It would be interesting to inquire whether or not this is the result of over-civilization, of a meticulous cultivation of the essential artificialities of existence. Assuredly it is not barbarian. In any consideration of Arthur Symons it is impossible to escape a direct discussion of the man himself, for he is too evident in his work, too utterly revealing, too obviously an impressionist of his own days setting down his moods as they flutter through him, leaving nothing to imagination. No matter what Arthur Symons writes about in poetry, in the last analysis we discover that the subject is himself. He is eternally tearing the veils from his little temple.

His self-betrayals are not ungraceful, for we observe that the essential Arthur Symons is a creature of rhythm. He is a vibrating string upon which the period plays itself out until it is tired. And the period long ago became tired. Symons is the perfect product of the Yellow Nineties. He was the editor of its most representative organ, *The Savoy*. He was the man who brought Paul Verlaine to London. He was the poet of the city streets, of the music-halls, of the light o' loves — " the Juliet of a night," of the five senses. He was the essayist par excellence who revealed the period to itself. In his Paterian sentences he has expressed the very spirit of the 1890s. The period may have been colored by a certain flower extravagantly praised by the tragic comedian of Tite Street and the cover of a quarterly edited by Henry Harland, but beneath the artificial hues ran the deep rivers of an authentic spiritual mood. We are apt to lose sight of that fact when we turn back to the work of Symons, of Dowson, and the lesser men. They were artificial, yes, insofar as their work is a conscious revelation of themselves, and they worked to death the few strings that composed their instruments. The demon of sensual love, the frantic desire for material beauties, the painful self-tortures of the spirit, these things are evident in most of their writing, and it is equally evident that they have been consciously placed there. But is it possible to imagine them in different guises? Could Ernest Dowson, with his thin, pale, delicate strain and his ineffectual flinging of sad roses, have been in anywise different? He was the child of his period. And Arthur Symons was equally a child of the period except that we may guess that he was a little more conscious of his reasons for being of the period. Dowson was a natural product; Arthur Symons, on the contrary, was a cultivated product. He could explain to himself and to others why he was what he was. He could enunciate his own artistic credo with no small degree of clarity. To those who accused him of writing poetry that was unwholesome, that had a smell of Patchouli about it, he could write:

"Patchouli! Well, why not Patchouli? Is there any 'reason in nature' why we should write exclusively about the natural blush, if the delicately acquired blush of rouge has any attraction for us? Both exist; both, I think, are charming in their way; and the latter as a subject has, at all events, more novelty. If you prefer your 'new mown

77

hay' in the hayfield, and I, it may be, in a scent-bottle, why may not my individual caprice be allowed to find expression as well as yours? Probably I enjoy the hayfield as much as you do, but I enjoy quite other scents and sensations just as well and I take the former for granted and write my poems, for a change, about the latter."

One might retort to this that the true poet does not write poems for " novelty " or " for a change." He writes them to express himself. But this is just what Arthur Symons did, as he explained a bit farther on in this very same discussion of the virtues of Patchouli. He declared:

" . . . I prefer town to country; and in the town we have to find for ourselves, as best we may, the *décor* which is the town equivalent of the great natural *décor* of fields and hills. Here it is that artificiality comes in; and if anyone sees no beauty in the effects of artificial light in all the variable, most human, and yet most factitious town landscape, I can only pity him, and go on my own way."

What more may be said? Arthur Symons was a creature of the town, of lighted streets at night, of the blazing footlights and the flashing skirts behind them, of scented meetings at stage-doors, of perfumes and jewels and lingerie and rings and rouge and patchouli and hansoms and all the divine tawdry intoxication of sophistication. In no man's poetry has this phase of life been more colorfully, more

78

melodiously revealed. And because his choice was deliberate we cannot affirm that it was not sincere. The light drew the moth and he needs must flutter about the dangerous, desirous flame. In his own words Arthur Symons made his choice.

ROSA MUNDI

An angel of pale desire
Whispered me in the ear
(Ah me, the white-rose mesh
Of the flower-soft, rose-white flesh!)
"Love, they say, is a fire:
Lo, the soft love that is here!

"Love, they say, is a pain
Infinite as the soul,
Ever a longing to be
Love's, to infinity,
Ever a longing in vain
After a vanishing goal.

"Lo, the soft joy that I give
Here is the garden of earth;
Come where the rose-tree grows,
Thine is the garden's rose,
Weave rose-garlands, and live
In ease, in indolent mirth."

Then I saw that the rose was fair,
And the mystical rose afar,
A glimmering shadow of light,
Paled to a star in the night;
And the angel whispered, "Beware,
Love is a wandering star.

79

Love is a raging fire,
Choose thou content instead;
Thou, the child of the dust,
Choose thou a delicate Lust."
"Thou hast chosen!" I said
To the angel of pale desire.

This is no love of calmness, but the fevered passion of sophisticated places. And Love to Arthur Symons did not mean one strong passion. He was in love with Love and he followed his wandering star through many fragrant verses. And so we find his books, "Silhouettes," "London Nights," "Amoris Victima," "Images of Good and Evil," "Knave of Hearts" and "Lesbia and Other Poems" (the last two but echoes of the man) compact with wearied endeavor, with importunate traveling over the bright plains of passion. The period undoubtedly made him, but he was willingly malleable to that period. Many things made the period. France, the France of Paul Verlaine, of Stephane Mallarme, of Charles Baudelaire, of Olivier Metra's valses, of Yvette Guilbert's chansons, of La Melinite's bright heels and Nini Patte en L'Air's apricot-colored drawers and Manet's women, had something to do with it. Some of these influences were old and made a belated entrance, but they found an eager group to welcome them. The figures

80

of the Nineties pass like a strange phantasmagoria now, a monstrous procession of barbarously painted masks keeping step to heathenish flutes and drums. Heading the procession was Oscar Wilde, called by Symons " an artist in attitudes." And there was the thin and despairing figure of Ernest Dowson, the pallid prose of Hubert Crackanthorpe, the perverse drawings of Aubrey Beardsley, the dry cerebral passion of John Davidson. It was the era of bicycles and bloomers, of The Yellow Book and The Savoy, of Lottie Collins's red skirt and " Ta-Ra-Ra-Boom-De-Ay." Who remembers " Daisy Bell " and " After the Ball" ? What were Leonard Smithers and The Bodley Head publishing? Who was about to repent and join the Roman Catholic Church?

But there was more than that. Other influences were working their way in. There were Kipling and Shaw and Lionel Johnson and all the Irish group. The atmosphere was heavy with sulphurous fumes of an alien incense from France, but the England of Henley's young men, of William Watson, of even George Meredith, was still plunging on toward undiscovered goals. And in art there were William Rothenstein and Charles Conder to combat the influence of Beardsley. Phil May titillated the masses. Neither must Max Beerbohm be forgotten, even

81

though he was writing defences of cosmetics in those days.

The later work of Arthur Symons (that in " Lesbia and Other Poems," for instance) brings it all back, for he has stood still apparently while time has progressed He is as much *fin-de-siecle* now as he was in 1896. There may be many reasons for this. It is quite imaginable that the greater bulk of Arthur Symons's later poetry is fugitive work written long ago and now first collected for its pathetic embalming between covers. But the very gesture of publication shows that the man still stands beside the sad Horsel Hill of the Nineties. He has not changed his gods although the gods are dead. He keeps one flickering flame still feebly burning upon the deserted altar, an altar upon which the ashes long ago grew cold. And in the new light of reason, the hard cerebral glare of our own tremendous days, we may now perceive how vague and tenuous that flame is that once dazzled us so. It is a sad spectacle, for it shows the triumph of time and transitory things over a nature that was sensitively attuned to the most delicate vibrations and impressions. Yet there is a faint, far-off appeal in these outmoded verses; something compels us to an admiration which yet leaves our reason unmoved. There has been doubt as to whether Symons the poet would outlast Symons the prose-writer, but there can be no doubt but what the man's poetry is the man himself. The note is monotonously melancholy at times, but it is never insincere (with exceptions, of course) and never forced.

In examining this later poetry (if it be later poetry), certain consistencies are to be observed, the repetition of moods that had their genesis in the days of the green carnation. Above all things, the weariness of love persists, a love that fatigues the soul as well as the body. This fatigue has been called a malady of the soul by Symons himself. From it his spiritual dolours rise. It is the note of regret, a despairing regret for all beautiful and piteous and passing things. It is the sad acknowledgment that the women who have starred the dreamer's life must eventually become equal memories with the dead roses of yesteryear. The transcience of time obsesses this mood, for continually the ghosts of dead ideals come back to haunt the artist. The melancholy of Arthur Symons grows into a misty, Watteau-like sadness. It is as though someone were playing a tinkling air of Rameau on some old harpsichord in a room blue with the smokes of twilight. In " Dreams " he wails:

Tired out with grieving over love,
  Love once so kind, so cruel grown,
I wake into an alien day
  Of near oblivion.
The white dawn gathers, aching white:
Surely I had ill dreams last night?

For, lying drowsily awake,
  Desiring only to forget,
Remembered joys return in grief,
  Kisses remembered yet,
Her lips on mine, her lips now mine
No more, or now no more divine.

Breathed on and dimmed, that face still haunts
  The mirror of my memory;
Her face—but ah, it is these tears
  That hide her face from me.
Oh Memory, from my heart remove
Even the memory of love!

This is a mode that has become a thing of the
past now. The delicate sighs, the despairing gestures, the fragile dancers of " Fetes Galantes," the
desolate acceptance of the passing of beauty (so
true of the Nineties) have been transmuted to an
artificial attitude that no longer holds the reader.
Whether it is due to the renascence of Whitman's
influence, the elaborate experimentations with new
verse-forms, or the vitally aroused interest in contemporary life, the poet no longer turns wholly

within himself in this faintly-perfumed sentimental manner for his inspiration. He no longer sighs about his own moods. The approach is too cerebral now. Whether or not this is better for the future of poetry cannot be settled while we are in the midst of this new mode. It may be better. Then again, it may drive poetry into a stark, involved utterance that will hardly appeal to more than select coteries. Artificiality still has its place in poetry, but it has become an artificiality of utterance (*vide* the seven cantos of Mr. Ezra Pound, for instance), a hard cerebralism that does not simplify beauty as poetry did in the past. Once it was sufficient to merely touch the heart, to arouse ecstasy or sadness or triumph with melody and rare images. Now the brain must be touched as well. It is to be imagined that many of the modern poets are attempting to marry the heart and the brain. What will come of that strange wedding Time must show.

The symbolic significance of artificial things is strong in the work of Arthur Symons, but the symbolism is always simple. It is easily comprehended. One does not have to read " Sordello " as easily as Isaac Watts in order to grasp it. Rings, jewels, flowers, rouge, patchouli, music-halls, ballets, all the sophisticated sadnesses of passing time, cry out their

85

messages to him. It is a source of unceasing pity to him that beautiful things must go. He is so much a part of his world with all its temporal illusions that he cannot turn to the eternal things for any peace or comfort. He may declare that he sits weaving his worlds out of dreams, but we do not believe him. He constantly weaves the colored existence about him into his dreams, and when the bright threads fade he is desolate. Like Ernest Dowson, he is " desolate and sick of an old passion." Great memories come back to him in little things. He can build a spiritual tragedy about the cast-off things of a woman once loved.

> I know you by the voices of your rings:
> Unhappy and inevitable things
> Cry to me in their shining silence; each
> Has its own fatal and particular speech.
> There is a ring with rubies that I hate:
> You wear it often, and it lies in wait
> Like an assassin, shooting fire at me
> When your pale finger seeks it lingeringly.
> Two rings I watch for, hoping, half in dread,
> To see the one; but if I see instead,
> Worn on the third left finger, and alone,
> A certain poor old ring with a blue stone,
> I pity first myself, as lovers do,
> Then I forget all else, and pity you.

One virtue of this poetry is its complete identification with the singer. Especially is this true when Arthur Symons writes about places. Wherever he goes, and he has been in many strange and beautiful places, the spirit of the surroundings take hold of him and his mood is colored by it. Each city, each street of frowning or smiling houses, every beach that fronts the multitudinously-mooded sea, meadows of placid green and the bird-infested loneliness of woods, react upon him. His is a delicate organism quivering to the touch of time and place. Like some strange, delicate, mysterious instrument, he is played upon by his surroundings. The place translates itself into him and he translates himself into the place. He is the perfect impressionist.

Yet all this, charming and poignant as it is, becomes obscured with the fine white dust of Time. The mode has veered away from Arthur Symons and his fragile and piteous songs strike us as coldly as butterflies pinned to a sheet of cardboard. We note the beauty, the fragility, the iridescence of gossamer wings, but something vital is lacking. In no one poem has he risen to that fine ardor of desolate passion, that complete self-revelation of nature that is to be found in Ernest Dowson's " Non Sum Qualis Eram Bonæ Sub Regno Cynaræ." Yet he is an epi-

87

tome of the Nineties; his career is a history of that epoch, and in his essays (which are quite another side of his personality) he has better expressed the intellectual atmosphere of his day than any other writer. His day is gone, however, and he has lived beyond it. He remains the visual example of a period that lived not wisely but too well. In a last analysis, he is a ghost — a revenant of the Nineties.

SWINBURNE'S HOME LIFE

SWINBURNE'S HOME LIFE

HE home life of a genius is often so disappointing, so sedentary and uninspired a process of incubation that it is always wise to approach books that treat of such intimacies without too great a measure of expectation. This warning is hardly necessary to lovers of Swinburne, for his home life with Walter Theodore Watts Dunton at The Pines, Putney Hill, was no secret. Mrs. Watts Dunton's " The Home Life of Swinburne," if we except the hodge-podge of tea-table anecdotes and small talk which gives it a gossipy interest, brings hardly anything new to the subject. Watts Dunton's valiant rescue of the brandy-drinking pagan poet from a sick-bed in Great James Street and the nursing of that poet (a process that took thirty years) is ancient history. Most readers know all they need to know about the carefully regulated days at The Pines, and, indeed, Mrs. Watts Dunton's book proves that they know all that there was to know. The whole thing formulates itself into a rapidly ossifying brain and childlike existence that assuredly was not stemmed in any degree by Watts Dunton. It is impossible to assert at this late date that The Pines did, or did not, destroy Swinburne as a great poet. It may be true that he would have destroyed himself, anyway, if Watts Dunton had left him on his sick-bed in Great James Street. Indeed, evidence would seem to favor such a theory. Mrs. Watts Dunton is furious enough about those critics who have ascribed Swinburne's lessening vitality as a poet during the last thirty years of his life to the influence of Watts Dunton. " There is no chapter in literary history," she asserts, "dealing with men's friendships more lovely; and yet envy and spite have tried to disfigure the public aspect of this sweet and sacred thing."

In the past I have leaned toward the theory that Watts Dunton's influence on Swinburne was as bad mentally as it was good physically, and nothing that Mrs. Watts Dunton has to say in this volume would seem to shake that theory. She looked upon her husband apparently as a sort of reincarnation of Alfred Tennyson's good old Victorian King Arthur. He possessed toward Swinburne what Mrs. Watts Dunton quite rightly calls " the mothering instinct." She asserts of her husband: " His anxiety for his [Swinburne's] physical welfare, his great interest in his mental output, his concern for his domestic comfort and for his amusement were beautiful to witness." "Walter," she remarks in another place, "ruled him by love, guided him by advice, and influenced him by suggestion." All this, it must be remembered, is written about him who, as Max Beerbohm once put it, "erstwhile clashed cymbals in Naxos."

Now, there have been two theories prevalent concerning the sad debacle of Swinburne's later years. One is that the poet needed alcohol to whip his brain up to the proper point of ecstasy in order to write his greatest poetry, and this is the sole theory to which Mrs. Watts Dunton pays any attention. She is horrified at it, and quite properly so, for there is no proof that Swinburne wrote any of his greatest poetry while under the influence of alcohol. But the second theory is not disposed of so easily, and perhaps this is why Mrs. Watts Dunton ignores it. That theory is based on the premise that Swinburne's poetry fell off during his later years because Watts Dunton's stodgy mind began to permeate and influence the inspiration of the poet. Of course, Swinburne would not write about Faustine again with Walter's careful eye upon him. The poet had been set down in surroundings that made such a procedure impossible. He was in

93

a Victorian household where everything moved like
clockwork. He got up and breakfasted about ten
o'clock, read the daily paper, ambled about Wimbledon Common, drank a bottle of Bass at the Rose
and Crown, had luncheon, an afternoon nap, wrote
from four o'clock until six, read aloud until 7:45,
had dinner at eight, and then retired to his library.
And that for thirty years was the life of the man
who shifted the values of mid-Victorian poetry!
One can but regret Watts Dunton's " great interest
in his [Swinburne's] mental output " and the fact
that he guided the poet " by advice and influenced
him by suggestion."

Nothing but gratitude can be extended to Watts
Dunton for his activity in 1879, but it is to be regretted that it had to be Watts Dunton. His was
a calm, moderate, machine-like, critical mind, full
of the milk of human kindness, but hardly capable
of intensifying the vagaries of genius. Swinburne
did not live his own life at The Pines, whatever
Mrs. Watts Dunton may say. The evidence is too
strongly on the other side. The poet led Watts
Dunton's life. In spite of the dynamic qualities of
Swinburne's brain, it is obvious that he was weak
and easily dominated. He had no head for practi-
calities, and it was easier to let other people do

things for him than do them himself. And because
of this, because he took the line of least resistance,
was nursed back to health and then permitted himself to be coddled for the rest of his life, we have
the figure of the dapper little gentleman who would
observe the picture of a baby and coo, " Oh, the
little duck! Did you ever see such darling dimples?
Just look at those sweet little arms! Isn't he perfect?" Mrs. Watts Dunton, by the way, sets this
speech down with the utmost gravity.

Except for inconsequentialities and a number of
minor anecdotes of some interest, there is nothing
new in Mrs. Watts Dunton's volume except the
rather touching chapter recording the poet's last
days. Here she does reach a certain height of
poignancy, although, to be quite honest, she fumbles
it through an inveterate sentimentality which makes
itself manifest throughout the book. I do not remember that the last days of Swinburne have ever
been so minutely described before, and it may be of
some interest to set down part of Mrs. Watts Dunton's narrative. She writes:

"A nurse was stationed on the landing outside his
room with the door open, for in his lucid moments
it would have irritated him to see a strange woman

sitting by his bedside. Walter prepared both nurses for the possibility that their presence might excite their distinguished patient to the utterance of ' Elizabethan language,' and requested them not to go near him except when absolutely necessary. Upstairs in his room, although by now he was gaining strength, Walter lay in bed strained and nervous, wondering what the issue would be. At intervals I would go down to Swinburne to take little messages to him from Walter. I found that he absolutely refused to allow the nurse to administer oxygen. Though he was sometimes delirious, he was conscious enough to know that a stranger was bending over him, and when she attempted to place the tube near his mouth he beat it away with his hands, crying out in an enfeebled voice, ' Take it away, take it away! '

" But the nurse's science told her that oxygen was necessary, and accordingly Walter's influence was asked for and promptly used. Acting as Walter's proxy, I went to Swinburne's bedside and told him that Walter considered the oxygen to be akin to a sea breeze, and that it would do him all the good in the world. He opened his eyes and gladly allowed me to put the tube quite near his mouth as he inhaled the vapor without another murmur.

" It was painful sometimes to watch him hurl the blankets off his chest and shoulders as he tossed about in a state of high fever. No sooner had the nurse or I replaced them than he would again try to fling them off. Occasionally he would talk wildly for a long while without stopping. I remember the nurse asked me in what language he was talking. I could catch a word here and there as he muttered long sentences with astonishing rapidity, and an occasional phrase in his disjointed monologue made me guess that he was speaking or reciting in Greek."

It was in this manner, the victim of double pneumonia, that Swinburne died on the morning of April 10, 1909. It is pathetic to note that the dying poet, dreamer to the last, would take his oxygen only after it had been urged upon him as something akin to a sea breeze. He who had been a stormy petrel in his younger days never lost his passion for the sea.

The picture that Mrs. Watts Dunton draws of Swinburne as a bibliophile is pleasing, but it is hardly as arresting a portrait as that furnished some years ago by Max Beerbohm, who passed an afternoon with the poet among his rare first editions.

Swinburne's passions were few, and Mrs. Watts Dunton is careful to note them all. There was Victor Hugo, for instance, and there was Dickens.

Several pages are given over to a description of Swinburne as a reader of Dickens. He was a very bad reader, according to Mrs. Watts Dunton, although in later years she became rather fascinated by his delivery. It seems that Swinburne would attempt to convey character by the tones of his voice as he read, and, as the poet was far from being an actor, the attempt was generally a failure. His high falsetto voice must have been a surprising thing. Another enthusiasm was the blossoming hawthorns on Wimbledon Common, and great was Swinburne's excitement the season he wheedled Mrs. Watts Dunton into accompanying him on a trip of inspection to them. " I found that he knew each one separately and individually," writes Mrs. Watts Dunton, " as one knows old friends. He ran from one to another, jumping over the numerous intersecting dikes and ditches and giving me his hand to help me to leap over to his side. When he got to one large hawthorn of divine loveliness, he paused for a long time in front of it and drew in long, deep breaths, as though he were inhaling the subtle emanation of the blossoms he so rapturously adored, and softly and repeatedly ejaculated, ' Ah-h-h ! ' " And of course his enthusiasms for the sea and babies are repeatedly emphasized. One chapter deals al-

most wholly with efforts to find a likely shore resort
for the poet, and there is quite a pathetic touch in
the account of Swinburne's sad discovery that he
was getting too old to remain very long in the water.

Although unimportant, there is much to amuse
the reader in the two chapters concerning Swinburne's fads and his difficulties as a man of business.
He never would let a tailor measure him, because
he did not like the idea of foreign hands traveling
over his body. This necessitated all his suits being
cut from the one he possessed. Checks were an
abhorrence to him and he never cashed them, sometimes thrusting large ones away in odd corners,
where they remained hidden for months. He was
averse to carrying small coins, and this appears to
be part of his aristocratic heritage, for he feared
contamination from them. Christmas was a gala
time at The Pines, and many were the mysterious
proceedings on Swinburne's part as the holiday drew
near. He was meticulous in his selection of Christmas cards, and great was his delight when he discovered any with ships upon them.

Of all the people who came to visit Swinburne
but one is selected by Mrs. Watts Dunton for special
mention, and this proves to be the novelist, F.
Marion Crawford. Swinburne got on very well

with him, and so too, apparently, did Watts Dunton and his wife. Mrs. Watts Dunton even mentions such trivial things as Swinburne's predilection for blue writing paper and for Samphire Soap. She informs us that his newspaper was the *Daily Telegraph*, there being "too much 'We-ishness' about the *Times*." Although Mrs. Watts Dunton is careful to state that Swinburne was not eccentric, it is hard to resist a smile at her description of the poet's appearance. He braced his trousers so high, she asserts, that he showed several inches of white sock. "Furthermore, he had a curious prancing gait, and his deliberate way of flinging out his feet before him as he trod the ground reminded one of a dancing master or a soldier doing the goose-step."

An entire chapter is devoted to the bard's humor, but the evidences of it offered are pretty sad. For instance, Mrs. Watts Dunton covers a lot of paper describing one anecdote which culminates in the fact that Swinburne read "Walter Watts" into the obituary of "Richard Watts" in Dickens's "The Seven Poor Travelers." There is nothing brilliant in this, and as one looks through the book, observing the various remarks ascribed to Swinburne, one wonders at the dullness of the poet. We have Mrs. Watts Dunton's word for it that he scintillated at times and that his excoriations were fearsome and wonderful to hear, but there are certainly no examples of any such wit or excoriations to be discovered in the book. One cannot but reach the conclusion that the author of " The Home Life of Swinburne " has left much unsaid and has carefully selected those few tidbits of information with which she does interlard her appreciation of the poet. In no sense of the word does this volume close the door to *the* biography of Swinburne. Edmund Gosse did not do it, and neither does Mrs. Watts Dunton. Of course, the hostess of The Pines is attempting no such thing, but even the ground which she has selected for herself is so meagerly scraped at as to make it imperative that an authentic history of those last thirty years be yet written. It must be remembered that she did not become a part of the menage at The Pines until the very fag-end of Swinburne's life, and much of her observation was made through the eyes of a girl, and a girl very much in love with Theodore Watts Dunton at that. It was but natural that she should have seen Swinburne through the eyes of her husband.

Certain sillinesses creep into the book. For instance, there is the gravely delivered information that Swinburne carefully folded up his napkin after a meal. Did Mrs. Watts Dunton imagine that her readers would jump to the conclusion that the poet flung it upon the floor after he had satisfied his appetite? It is easy to perceive why certain people have asserted that this volume is in bad taste. It is really not so, for the enthusiasm and undoubted love for the poet of the woman who wrote it lift it from any such quagmire. But it does have its lapses, and a rather serious one is the unconscious belittlement of Swinburne that runs through it. It is a loving belittlement, but it is insidious. It strips and presents as absolutely helpless a character that must have possessed many sound masculine traits. True enough, Swinburne's anger is hinted at, but, being hinted at, it is quickly slurred over. Mrs. Watts Dunton is striving to place a halo on a head that had been haloed long before she was born, and with a flaming halo that she can hardly comprehend. There is no doubt that the young pagan Swinburne gradually metamorphosed into the quaint little Victorian gentleman who never ran far from his masculine nursemaid, Watts Dunton, but there is hardly any need to rub it in so vigorously.

There is a psychological problem implicit in the career of Swinburne that will be worked out some day, and it is safe to assert that Mrs. Watts Dunton's volume will prove valuable at that time. And it will prove valuable, not for the conscious information she gives, but for the unconscious betrayals which she does not perceive and never will be able to perceive.

W. H. HUDSON

W. H. HUDSON

T was Mr. J. C. Squire who wronged both himself and the late W. H. Hudson in a discussion of the English naturalist's prose style. Besides showing himself rather out of tune with Hudson's crystal clarity, he also showed himself a poor judge. The *Observer* carried Mr. Squire's appraisal, and a paragraph of it may be set down as establishing a position from which the present writer may politely but emphatically remove himself. Mr. Squire declared:

" For Mr. Hudson's English very seldom failed. The style being the man, the style had limitations. The man's love for nature burned with a steady and equable radiance; he drank, if you like, perpetually from that fountain, but never to intoxication. He seldom felt like rhapsodizing; he never came near swooning with esthetic delight nor was taken up in religious exaltation. Spirit and sense were always awake in him, but temperate in their enjoyments. Add his general lack of humor and his proclivity toward retrospection and regret and you get naturally something like a dead-level of writing. For a man who wrote so much and so well he produced very few ' memorable pages.' The anthologists who hunt for purple passages of prose will find that he constantly baffles them; one page is so like another, and when they like two sentences they will not want the third, which will very likely change the subject. He had the defects of his qualities and the qualities of his defects. He wrote carefully; his constructions are clear and his epithets accurate. Beyond that the deliberate artificer did not often go. He was preoccupied with his matter; he wrote about certain things in a certain mood, and took no pains to play upon the eyes and ears of his readers. One looks through his style as through glass — slightly tinted glass — at the objects behind it; and his loveliest passages as a rule are simply those in which the loveliest objects are mentioned."

This paragraph is quoted in Edward Garnett's " Note on Hudson's Literary Art," to be found prefixed to the new edition of " Nature in Downland." Mr. Garnett, however well disposed as he is toward Hudson's work, does not refute Mr. Squire's passage with the vigor it deserves, albeit he does slightingly mention the English critic's " magisterial finality." Mr. Squire is absolutely wrong. There is no dead level in Hudson's prose. One need but compare " Nature in Downland " and

" El Ombu " and "A Crystal Age " to confirm this statement. The style in " British Birds " is not the same style to be found in " Fan: The Story of a Young Girl's Life." What Hudson did was to adapt his style to his subject. As for " purple passage," there are no such flares as Pater's description of the Mona Lisa to be found, because Hudson was not that kind of writer. He was essentially a restrained observer, and even his remembered emotions are set down in tranquility. It is true that there is a deal of retrospect in his work, but what reason is there to speak of this in a slighting tone? It was not a monotonous mumbling, but a clear and beautiful recapturing of great days, of days on the Pampas, along the La Plata, in English highways, in the very streets of London.

The reason for this continued retrospection is obvious. Hudson was continually writing about himself, about his reactions to nature. He was probably the most personal writer of his time. Even in the romances, in " Green Mansions," in the vivid tales of "El Ombu," in the topographical romance of " The Purple Land," he was drawing on the marvelous reservoir of his own life for details and impressions. Before one finds this monotonous or a " dead level," one must agree that Hudson's life was uninteresting and also a " dead level." That it was far from that the most cursory reader must know. Because his last days were days of quiet pilgrimages to small English towns and villages, were wanderings in woodland glades and tiny roads, there is no reason to affirm that they were uninteresting. Indeed, those days were always vital with life and beauty. He was a calm mirror upon which was reflected the dreamlike epics of the hedges, the odysseys of small birds. Beneath his careful pen and keen eye the apparent calm of the green places became a clustering growth of beauty continually fretted with an intense pulse of life. We can hardly go through the pages of " Idle Days in Patagonia," " Nature in Downland," and " The Purple Land " without drinking in this beauty with an inexhaustible thirst. Just what Mr. Squire means by " He had the defects of his qualities and the qualities of his defects " is not clear in this particular application, however superficially witty the phrase may seem. It means nothing, the case with most epigrammatic statements. In fact, it might be applied to any writer. We all have the defects of our qualities and the qualities of our defects. Even Mr. Squire.

But enough of Mr. Squire. He has served to open the gate to Hudson's work, and that is enough.

In searching my mind for material with which to describe Hudson's style (not the style of " Birds in London " and " British Birds," which were written particularly for naturalists, and are necessarily meticulous description), two small episodes (both connected with Hudson's work) appear. One was an adventure with a bird while reading "Afoot in England " in the country one Spring ago. It was a robin who gravely hopped within three feet of me, placed his head on one side and viewed me for a long time with a bright, beady eye. Then it twisted its head the other way and viewed me with the other eye. It seemed perplexed, wondering what a lummox like myself was doing in its own particular green field. Then it uttered a long, clear whistle, a delicious liquid-like note, and fluttered away. At the moment I was reading Hudson's description of his pilgrimage to the monoliths at Stonehenge, his objective being to see the sun rise over these mysterious ruins and note the shadows cast by the stones. The robin's whistle chimed with the paragraph, and I thought, " This is Hudson's style — the sweet notes of the robin." And, indeed, as one goes through his books the impression rises that he writes as easily as a bird sings, that his art is the greatest of art because it is so artless, so spontaneous, so clearly

111

cadenced. Joseph Conrad declared that Hudson " writes as the grass grows." " You can't tell how this fellow gets his effects." Neither can you tell how a bird gets its effects.

Later that same day I went to bathe my hot face in a small stream and, stooping down, I thought how clear the water was, how I could see the pebbles with surprising clarity, and how the tiny tadpoles appeared to be swimming in air instead of liquid. Here again is Hudson's style, a clear, pellucid, crystal-like magic. In reading his descriptions of nature we seem less to be noting his words than gazing through his eyes. He makes us see just what he desires, and how is it possible for him to do this without a rare selection of matter and a magic comprehension. This vividness of description, this magic of making his eyes our own, can be illustrated from Hudson's work, in spite of Mr. Squire's declaration that when the anthologists " like two sentences they will not want the third, which will very likely change the subject." Let us take for example the wounded eagle in " Idle Days in Patagonia." Hudson desired a Magellanic eagle-owl, and finding one, he prepared to kill it. In Mr. Hudson's words:

" I fired, he swerved on his perch, remained suspended for a few moments, then slowly fluttered down.   Behind the spot where he had fallen was a great mass of tangled dark-green grass, out of which rose the tall, slender boles of the trees; overhead through the fretwork of leafless twigs the sky was flushed with tender roseate tints, for the sun had now gone down and the surface of the earth was in shadow.   There, in such a scene, and with the wintry quiet of the desert over it all, I found my victim, stung by his wounds to fury and prepared for the last supreme effort.   Even in repose he is a big, eagle-like bird; now his appearance was quite altered, and in the dim, uncertain light he looked gigantic in size — a monster of strange form and terrible aspect.   Each particular feather stood out on end, the tawny barred tail spread out like a fan, the immense tiger-colored wings wide open and rigid, so that as the bird, that had clutched the grass with his great feathered claws, swayed his body from side to side — just as a snake about to strike sways his head, or as an angry, watchful cat moves its tail — first the tip of one, then of the other wing touched the ground.   The black horns stood erect, while in the centre of the wheel-shaped head the beak snapped incessantly, producing a sound resembling the click of a sewing machine.   This was a suitable setting for the pair of magnificent furious eyes, on

113

which I gazed with a kind of fascination, not un-mixed with fear when I remembered the agony of pain suffered on former occasions from sharp, crooked talons driven into me to the bone. The irises were of a bright orange color, but every time I attempted to approach the bird they kindled into great globes of quivering yellow flame, the black pupils being surrounded by a scintillating crimson light, which threw out minute yellow sparks into the air. When I retired from the bird this preternatural fiery aspect would instantly vanish."

How can anybody read this without being thrilled? And how can anybody call this a " dead level" of writing? Hudson is equally fine in his descriptions of nature, and one of his most touching aspects is the manner in which he communicates his own mood to the scene and how the scene colors him. Nature, vast plains, mountains blue lined against the distance, the riotous colors of tropical flowers and fruits, deep ravines in which the shadows eternally huddle, all these things fling their magic about Hudson and he instantly identifies himself with them. Whether it be South America or England, he plunges into the natural atmosphere about him as a swimmer does into deep waters and it colors his mind, his eyes, his brain. Yet, in spite

114

of this passion, he is always master of his pen; he co-ordinates his impressions and conveys them with rare dexterity to the reader. The accusation that he never swoons with esthetic delight may be true if by that is meant that he never grows incoherent or loses mastery of his instrument; but he feels the world as a bright, many-hued sea continually surging over him. There is a religious exaltation in his pages. It runs like a subterranean river beneath the smooth fabric of his prose, constantly bursting through and manifesting itself in thoughts of eternity. In "Idle Days in Patagonia" there is a description of the plains of Patagonia from which a brief section may be removed to illustrate how closely Hudson identifies himself with the particular terrain over which he is traveling. The whole chapter is an admirable presentation of Hudson at his best, but even the following paragraph will give a fair idea of his sure command of style:

"Everywhere through the light, gray mold, gray as ashes of myriads of generations of dead trees, where the wind had blown on it or the rain had washed it away, the underlying yellow sand appeared, and the old, ocean-polished pebbles, dull red, and gray, and green, and yellow. On arriving at a hill I would slowly ride to its summit, and stand

115

there to survey the prospect. On every side it stretched away in great undulations, but the undulations, were wild and irregular; the hills were rounded and cone-shaped, they were solitary and in groups and ranges; some sloped gently, others were ridge-like and stretched away in league-long terraces, with other terraces beyond; and all alike were clothed in the gray, everlasting, thorny vegetation. How gray it all was! Hardly less so near at hand than on the haze-wrapped horizon, where the hills were dim and the outline blurred by distance. Sometimes I would see the large, eagle-like, white-breasted buzzard, Buteo crythronotus, perched on the summit of a bush half a mile away; and so long as it would continue stationed motionless before me my eyes would remain involuntarily fixed on it, just as one keeps his eyes on a bright light shining in the gloom; for the whiteness of the hawk seemed to exercise a fascinating power on the vision, so surpassingly bright was it by contrast in the midst of that universal, unrelieved grayness."

In such prose as this do we find Hudson limning nature for us. No naturalist who has ever lived has brought us so closely to the wild itself, has impressed more indelibly upon our city-dimmed eyes the loneliness and vastness and strange sorcery of unexpected places and the wild creatures of the world. It takes a great imagination to do this, an imagination that must do more than content itself with retrospection and description. There is a creative instinct at work here that is only secondary to an overwhelming love of nature. Hudson, I believe, was at his best in the actual description of things seen, but he also produced a series of volumes in which the creative instinct was dominant and which hold very high rank among the greatest achievements of modern novels. "Green Mansions" has already been widely praised. Such men as John Galsworthy noted its beauty and made for it an important place among modern books. So too, have the short stories in "El Ombu" received their meed of praise.

But what shall be said of "A Crystal Age," Hudson's own idea of Utopia? It is a book that was written many years ago and the foibles of the 1880's are treated in it, but as a book of imagination it is compact with rare beauty and distinguished style. The scene of the book is clever and the picture drawn of the family in the far-away crystal age rings with a surprising authenticity. It is not such a Utopia as H. G. Wells might dream of, for science and inventions play no part in it. Rather

than that it is an existence where one lives only for
art and beauty, where all love one another with a
tender passion, where sex is unknown and where
only one woman in each great house, the Mother
of the House, procreates and makes possible the
endurance of the race. With what beauty and ideal-
ism all this is painted! The narrator of the tale,
having recovered from a bad fall into a ravine,
comes to himself in this new world and the story of
his gradual education to the new order of things,
the rarifying of his spirit, is carried on in a tender,
lucid manner that steadily mounts to the high tragic
moment of its finale when the man who has been
born again destroys himself for love of the angel-
like woman he feels can never be really his. Sadly
enough, his destruction comes at the moment when
this woman has been made Mother of the House
and she is about to take him as her own.

The world described is one in which we may guess
Hudson himself would desire to dwell. It is his
ideal land, a land in which all our petty institutions
have been consumed to even less than a memory —
politics, religions, systems of philosophy, 'isms and
'ologies of all descriptions, schools, churches, pris-
ons, poorhouses, stimulants, tobacco, kings, parlia-
ments, cannon, pianos, history, the press, vice, politi-

cal economy, money — everything. Nothing is left but a sweet freedom where men and women dress in aesthetic robes, go about their tasks such as plowing, pass the evenings in song — a music beyond our comprehension. Even in this land of the imagination Hudson is meticulous in his descriptions of nature and a wild, free, primeval terrain is spread before the reader. This is phantasy of the highest sort, so charmingly written as to hold the reader to the final tragic page.

Of course, Hudson has not always been as happy in his choice of material for fiction. "Fan: The Story of a Young Girl's Life," for instance, can hardly be regarded as a success in spite of its strong passages and frequent pages of excellent writing. This book was patiently written under the influence of George Gissing, for it is a tale of a slums child, and it employs all the frequent accessories which go with these tales, saloons, beaten mothers, etc. It was a strange experiment for Hudson and one views it with some amazement at first. Much more important is "Ralph Herne," which has just been made available in a most beautiful format. This short novel takes the reader back to that colorful South America that Hudson knows so well. Ralph Herne is a young struggling doctor who goes to

Buenos Ayres to set up practice. He finds he must wait and study Spanish before he can put out his shingle and, to his great despair, after a year of hard study, he fails. The result is that he loses his grip on himself and goes from bad to worse until he is brought up sharp by the girl he loves and whom he imagines is promised to another. After that Ralph redeems himself when an epidemic runs riot in the city. The construction of this book is faulty, and it must take a lesser place among Hudson's works, but, even at that, it is a distinguished piece of writing. The tender, whimsical, clarid style lifts the theme and the careful characterization adds immeasurable value to the tale. During the latter portion of the tale, where the horrors of the plague are described and the woman whom Ralph Herne loves falls a victim, there is a high sense of melodramatic vigor. The paragraphs slip swiftly by, imprinting upon the reader's mind a clear picture of this heart-breaking struggle between life and death.

In spite of Hudson's frequent excursions into fiction and the triumphs of " Green Mansions " and " El Ombu," we must regard the author as essentially a naturalist. That was his true function, and in it he labored more wisely than any other naturalist before him. He may not have been a great specialist

120

or even a final authority on his beloved birds, but he conveys his knowledge to his readers in such a manner as to make him more important to them than many a more portentous name. Somewhere in his work he remarks: " When we write, we do, as the red man thought, impart something of our souls to the paper." Assuredly this sentence might apply to Hudson himself. His soul shines from every page. His calm, gentle, eager spirit, always animated by the multifarious aspects of natural beauty, rises from every paragraph that he has ever written. In some aspects he is a writer's writer, for they alone can comprehend him at his full value. To them will come the wonder of these apparently artless sentences which yet convey so much and travel so far through the mind. How he wrote is a puzzle. It may have sprung up within him as the grass grows, and one likes to believe that. Certainly one reason for his excellence rests in the complete way in which he identified himself with the subject in hand. He felt strongly (we may never doubt that) and the very spirit must have animated the pen. He took the world to his breast and it responded with that tender, wholehearted ardor that the world always gives to those who fall passionately in love with it. Even in those books written primarily for students, books such as " The Naturalist in La Plata," " Birds in London " and " British Birds," this great love frequently reveals itself in shining crystal sentences. He belonged as wholly to nature as a woodland creature, and part of his charm lies in the gracious gestures with which he admitted his happy serfdom.

LAFCADIO HEARN

LAFCADIO HEARN

IRST of all, we must recognize the fact that Lafcadio Hearn was a cosmopolite, for that recognition in itself illuminates many of the peculiarities that make his literary work so unusual and distinctive. His father was a British Army officer, his mother was a Greek; he was born on Leucadia, one of the Ionian islands, and his early childhood was passed in England. Surely such a heterogeneous introduction to a life which was passed under the most trying difficulties could not but shape the oddly imaginative mind of Hearn into a strange and exotic form. Even the period of time which he did pass in the United States was colored by foreign influences. This is not so much the case during the Cincinnati and Philadelphia residences, but certainly the years spent in New Orleans and the two years in the West Indies can hardly be dubbed natively American. And the final and passing years of his life found Hearn in Japan, a country in which his genius flowered at its fullest and whose strangely ghostlike mysticism met a spontaneous response from the writer and teacher.

Besides bearing in mind the cosmopolitan nature of Hearn (he really belonged to no country), one must also remember the disadvantages under which he labored. IIe was practically blind; one eye was entirely so and the other possessed but a twentieth part of the normal vision. When writing, he was compelled to place the paper but three inches from his eye. And his blind eye was deformed, so much so that it disfigured his face. Recognizing these two facts, it can hardly be doubted that readers of Hearn's work will be better able to understand the achievements of the writer. Those achievements have at length (eighteen years after his death) been brought together in a uniform set that is a delight to the eye and a pleasure to read. For the first time we have "The Writings of Lafcadio Hearn" in a library edition that peculiarly adapts itself to a consideration of the writer's work as a whole. Hearn's work falls into three classifications: (1) His early fantastic and gruesome studies, (2) his color-splashed narratives of the French West Indies and old New Orleans, and (3) the large group of books on Japanese subjects upon which, properly speaking, his fame rests.

The early work (at least a portion of it, for much of that ancient matter is buried in the oblivion of

newspaper files) may be found under the titles,
" Leaves from the Diary of an Impressionist,"
" Creole Sketches," " Stray Leaves from Strange
Literature " and " Fantastics and Other Fancies."
Part of it is observation; another part, loose translation and rewriting and the rest of a creative order.
A wild luxuriance of fancy, splashed with riotous
color, a macabre romanticism that almost suggests
Hoffman, and a deliberate wallowing in gruesomeness for the sake of gruesomeness, mark these early
efforts. Wherever there was color or unusual ex-
oticism the myopic eye of Hearn was turned. And
this is remarkable when we consider that physically
he could see but a small portion of all this radiance
and stirring of savage hues. His imagination possessed a sombre and barbaric quality that needed but
a hint to rush frantically on in the most demonstra-
tive manner. This very fact renders some of his
early prose rather artificial and forced, but at its
best — in stray passages and odd fragments — it
rises to a height that challenges comparison with
De Quincey.

Hearn was not as great a stylist as De Quincey;
neither was he as fine an intellect; but at times he
made a near approach to the plane of that dark
English genius. The series of sketches which he

127

contributed week after week to a New Orleans paper are marked by this rich quality. Most of these sketches were the result of an intensive reading in exotic literature; indeed, many of the pieces were direct translations or paraphrases. Hearn was feeling for his proper metier. He was striving to orientate himself in a world of letters, and in this country he could find nothing that would quicken his pulses. So he dredged all the dark byways of letters, hauling up such monstrous lumber as subjects from Egyptian papyrus, from Indian and Buddhist literature, from Moslem tales. The strange, the bizarre, the uniquely sombre made their violent appeal to him, and his morbid fancy answered. The macabre qualities of Hearn's fancy had already manifested themselves in the days when he was a reporter in Cincinnati. Such news stories as his description of the tanyard murder case, which he wrote for *The Cincinnati Enquirer* (a piece of reporting, by the way, which may be regarded as the beginning of his literary career), give an excellent example of the darkness of his fancy and its delight in ghoulish investigation. But it must always be remembered that this trait (often pronounced in young romantic writers) was speedily brought under check, and while it is to be felt in back of his work even as late as such Japanese volumes as " Kotto " and " Kwaidan," it is restrained and occupies but its proper place. For a time a legend lingered in Cincinnati regarding Hearn's " vocabulary of the gruesome." One need but read his report of the tanyard murder to understand why.

Before Hearn left New Orleans for that epochal hegira to the French West Indies he had written a short novel (or novelette), entitled " Chita: A Memory of Last Island." The first version of this tale appeared in *The New Orleans Times-Democrat* under the title of " Torn Letters," and later it was lengthened and published as a serial in *Harper's Magazine* under the title by which it is known today. This story is among the most popular of Hearn's works, and there is good reason, for it is a beautifully written tale. Hearn secured his first real recognition with this story, and it was because of it that *Harper's Magazine* commissioned him to go on with those articles that resulted in " Two Years in the French West Indies." " Chita " is important in more ways than one. It was Hearn's first lengthy attempt at fiction, at genuine creative work. The plot is inconsequential; but it is not for the action that one reads " Chita." It is for the admirable capturing of atmospheric effects, for the delicate

129

development of character and for the strange music of the prose. Hearn needed but a hint and he was off for pages of the most exquisite writing. By this time he had combed his style sufficiently to remove from it those grotesqueries that had deformed the earlier works.

It is with " Chita," perhaps, that the first phase of Hearn's genius may be said to have reached a splendid finish, although certain critics insist on classifying the book with the West Indies novel, which followed after a short period. Mention has already been made of a large number of translations which are not included in the collected edition of his works. For one thing, he translated several of Gautier's more famous stories, among them being " One of Cleopatra's Nights." Then there were a series of Creole proverbs published under the title of " Gombo Zhebes." Later on in his life (1890) came a translation of Anatole France's " The Crime of Sylvestre Bonnard." However, it is the Gautier translations that are of importance here as intimating Hearn's fondness for the exotic in romance. He must have been an assiduous reader of French letters, and there are times in his work when we detect the influence of both Gautier and Flaubert. He could never quite reach the high plane of carefully restrained prose made famous by Flaubert, but he did touch the colorful and riotous imagination of Gautier.

In the middle '80s Hearn began to weary of New Orleans. He had explored the Creole life to its utmost, had even, according to rumor, indulged in Voodoo ceremonies. He began to look about him for new places unworked by the literary artisan and divorced from the artificial society atmosphere of cities, an atmosphere which he always hated to the very end of his life.

It is not until we reach the second classification of Hearn's work that the writer stands boldly out as a serious personage, an unusual addition to letters, and a man to be observed with critical enthusiasm. This second phase is at its full flowering in two volumes, " Two Years in the French West Indies " and " Youma : The Story of a West Indian Slave." Both of them are remarkable demonstrations of the power of visualizing bizarre people and tropical scenery. It was in 1887 that Hearn left New Orleans and settled at St. Pierre, Martinique. His imaginative faculties had long before enchanted him with dreams of that colorful land. He found his dream at first, for in a letter written soon after his arrival he declared : " I am absolutely bewitched,

131

and resolved to settle down somewhere in the West Indies. Martinique is simply heaven on earth. You must imagine a community whose only vices are erotic. There are no thieves, no roughs, no snobs. Everything is primitive and morally pure — except in the only particular where purity would be out of harmony with natural conditions."

The labors that were the result of his West Indies life are among the finest in his career. " Two Years in the French West Indies " is a volume (rather two volumes), of travel - pictures, personality sketches, and anecdotes fairly splashed in sunlight and beauty. The matter displays at its finest that rare power possessed by Hearn for getting under the skin of a foreign people, of setting down in print the very atmosphere of strange places. It is the power that makes the Japanese books of so great a beauty and charm. The fictional attempt made by Hearn as a result of these care-free days in Martinique should, perhaps, be considered with " Chita." " Youma " is a tragedy written with the utmost delicacy and care for tender detail. It displays Hearn's creative powers at their finest, for it is a better book than " Chita." The charm and color of West Indian skies glow through the tale and the final scene in the burning building is handled with the art of a master. However, in spite of the promise of " Chita " and the certain amount of achievement discoverable in "Youma," Hearn never was, in the true sense of the word, a creative artist. He depended on other material and observation. His finest accomplishment was the translation of exotic atmospheres into prose that drenches the reader in color.

With his departure to Japan in 1890 the great period of Hearn's life began. The books that were the result of that residence (a residence during which he became a Japanese citizen with the name of Yakumo Koisumi, married a Japanese wife and had children) belong to the major classifications of literature. These volumes, inspired by Japan, books such as " Glimpses of Unfamiliar Japan," " Out of the East," " Kokoro," " In Ghostly Japan," " Shadowings," " Kotto " and " Kwaidan," are marked by certain kindred impulses. There is more spirit than material observation in them. They retell in the most delicate manner legends, ghost stories, gentle habits and spiritual beliefs. They bring vividly before the reader the inward aspects of Shintoism and Buddhism. In other words, Hearn was translating the Japanese spirit for his American and English readers; he was never writing travel books. Even in his " Japan: An Attempt at Interpretation," the last book he wrote, he is not successful in interpreting the material aspects of an Oriental land. It is the spirit again, the strange medley of mysticism, superstition, and delicacy that make up the soul of the Japanese people. Such an objective required a most penetrating and understanding sympathy of nature, together with an instinctive understanding of spiritual nuances, and these attributes Hearn assuredly had. He was probably happier than he had ever been before (at least during the first decade of his residence in Japan), and this smoothing out of spirit is observable in his books. It was a calmer man writing, a contemplative individual who was absorbing the meditative detachment of the Oriental. The old unrest which expressed itself in a violent portrayal of gruesomeness had faded into a mystical absorption in ghostliness, a ghostliness that was rarefied. It is only in " Kotto " and " Kwaidan " that the gruesome strain begins to manifest itself again, and even there it is tinged by an Oriental strangeness. It is not quite the same.

He had faults of discursiveness, of lack of logic and construction, of occasional over-writing, but these things hardly interfere with the excellence of his best books. And there the reader will discover

134

a high literary excellence, together with a power of psychological analysis and sympathetic understanding, that has, among other things, brought the spirit of Japan closer to the Occidental. Hearn is essentially a creator of what Walter Pater termed " the delicacies of literature."

YIDDISH LITERATURE, AND THE
CASE OF SHOLOM ASCH

YIDDISH LITERATURE, AND THE
CASE OF SHOLOM ASCH

IDDISH literature is quite distinct from and more than a mere branch of that great flood of Hebrew writings that dates from the Old Testament and the Talmud. Although the first recognizable Hebrew book printed in this country (" Abne Joshua," New York, 1860) dates from the beginning of the Civil War, one must skip to the 'eighties before Yiddish letters proper make their appearance here. Then the writers, in a majority of cases lyric poets, spring up in abundance. It is no part of an article treating a single contemporary figure to do more than mention the beginnings of Yiddish letters and indicate briefly the authors who stand out as preeminent and lead directly to Sholom Asch. Three men who precede Asch, both chronologically and in the development of certain genres, should be noted, for it was mainly by their efforts that Yiddish prose grew into so admirable a reservoir of literary treasure. Sholom Abramovitch, known among his people as " the Jewish Cervantes," may be regarded as the first

139

complete fruition of the distinguished Yiddish writer, although he was born as late as 1836. Following him is Isaac Lob Peretz (born in 1851), whose tales and poems are still eagerly read. The third writer is Shalom Aleichem (Sholom Rabinovitch), who is possibly the best known of the older Yiddish writers to English readers. These men pictured Jewish life with humor and a keen sense of reality, a heritage that is being splendidly carried on today by Sholom Asch.

A group of younger people, comparatively speaking, grew up under the influence of these men and have, in many cases, already made a definite impress on Yiddish letters. Among them may be noted Abraham Reisen, Morris Rosenfeld, " Yehoash " (Solomon Bloomgarden), " Schomer " (Nahum Meyer Schaikewitz), Jacob Gordin, Leon Kobrin, Moishe Nadir, David Pinski, Abraham Cahan, and " Tashrak " (Israel J. Levin). These names are picked almost at random, and one is embarrassed at the names left out. The soil is exceedingly rich and no attempt has been made by the writer to cover it with any degree of adequacy. It is with Sholom Asch particularly that this article has to deal.

When Moishe Nadir affirmed that Sholom Asch possessed the holiday spirit, I misinterpreted him and wondered how Nadir, a Yiddish writer who must be accepted with all seriousness by anyone attempting to grasp the hugeness and quality of the Jewish literary output in America, could ascribe such a spirit to the author of " The God of Vengeance," " Mottke, the Vagabond," and " Uncle Moses." Rather did I find an ache in these books, the insistent voice of a coherent Jewish nationality manifesting itself in the face of a thousand obstacles. It was only after I had met and talked with Sholom Asch that I understood the deepness of Nadir's analysis. He meant that Asch possessed to a high degree the Jewish religious holiday spirit. Throughout his work, unfortunately so inaccessible in English, is to be found that fervor which foreign lands may not weaken, that pride untempered by reason and yet so admirable, that delight in the unity of the Jew all over the world. He is proud of the Jew as a Jew. And in the long annals of the Jews' obstinate persistence to retain their identity and not be devoured by the races that literally engulfed them, he finds much of his inspiration.

" It is the spirit of the Jewish faith kept alive throughout the ages," cries Asch, his face lighting up and his hands eagerly gesticulating, " that I must describe."

My first meeting with him was in the news room of the New York Jewish daily, the *Forward*. Later we repaired to a small restaurant but a few doors from noisy, picturesque East Broadway, where the Yiddish newspapers are huddled so closely together. One trait, thoroughly European, is possessed by the Jewish *litterateurs*. They love to foregather in a common place, to meet and mingle constantly with one another. It is the clique spirit of writers, so familiar in Paris and so alien to the more diffident self-consciousness of the Anglo-Saxon. The conversation is not particularly about books or work to be done. It represents rather a relaxation of mood. It is the atmosphere (poor overworked word!) which counts, that invigorating sense that the men sitting about are intellectual workers. There is incentive in this, a sensation that one must earn his right to mingle familiarly with this gathering. Perhaps herein lies one reason why the Yiddish writers are so everlastingly immersed in their projects, so set upon achievement. A bohemian note creeps in, although it is rather diluted by the glasses of astoundingly hot tea that compose the solitary liquid refreshment. Legend has it that the cafe where these men formerly met went out of business because the writers came there, sat all afternoon over one

142

or two glasses of tea, and then went away leaving
the aggrieved proprietor with an empty cash register. I doubt the wrath of the proprietor, though,
for I well remember being in a Jewish restaurant
with one or two writers and noting that the owner
effusively refused any payment whatsoever. This,
I was earnestly informed by Konrad Bercovici, however, was an exception.

Sholom Asch was generally to be found in the
cafe I have strayed so far from, at the luncheon
hour. He is a rather large man, tall and of substantial build. His prominent nose and small, neatly
cropped mustache suggest the typical business man
rather than the sensitive writer of novels and plays.
It is when his face lights up — and he smiles often
and most agreeably albeit a bit shyly — that his
features take on an intellectual aspect. His shyness
is somewhat accentuated by the care he takes in
selecting his English words. One must grasp at half
finished sentences to follow him with any degree of
success.

The fact that this man is famous among millions
of Jews is surprising when we take into consideration his age. Asch was born in Kutno, Poland, in
1880. Until he was sixteen or eighteen years old
he lived quietly at home, studying all the while. We

may guess that he was a bright boy at *cheder,* for his Jewish national sense has been an integral part of him since he could first comprehend it. Hebrew, as a study, was one of his first loves, and he has never forsaken it. Today he has to his credit a number of books in Hebrew as well as his more substantial successes in Yiddish. In an era when Hebrew is no more than a language of culture and Yiddish is the spoken tongue of a large portion of the people, this familiarity with the classic form is not so common as it may seem. Hebrew today appears to be assuming that place that Latin occupied in early church history. Most of the contemporary literature of the Jew is written in Yiddish, and we may guess that forty or fifty years ago the beginnings of a national literature in this tongue were not without opposition. It appears to be the old tale of writers eventually adopting the vulgar language of the masses in order to bring their works into the common home. All countries (except those as young as the United States) have passed through this phase. And even this country is building up a new and refreshing variant of the English language that would amaze Thackeray and Dickens. The tragedy of the Jew, however, appears to be that Yiddish is unstable and is already passing out. The young Jews speak

144

the language of the country wherein they reach
maturity. There are even pessimistic prophets
among the Jews who assert that it will not be
long before Yiddish goes the way of Hebrew and
becomes the spoken tongue of a pitifully small
minority.

In addition to acquiring Hebrew, Asch became a
student of German. When he was about eighteen
years old he went to live in Warsaw. Undoubtedly,
during those early years there he observed and put
away much of the material for " Mottke, the Vagabond." It was in Warsaw that he began to write.
The short story, the sketch, first absorbed his attention. He felt that through this medium he could
best give the multitude of thoughts and moods that
were seething in him. Always he has been a close
observer of his own people, and his work is, from
first to last, essentially realistic. As a young man
he was visibly influenced by the writings of Peretz.
When he was twenty-one years old he started in
quite seriously to carve out a literary career for
himself. He wrote numberless short stories, and,
due to the perspicacity of Abraham Cahan, his work
began to appear in Yiddish journals in America. It
is now fifteen years since Cahan began to print the
stories of Asch in the *Jewish Morning Journal.* Of

145

course, other papers followed suit, for editors had but to read his work to realize his value.

During his life Asch has traveled a great deal. Living in Austria, Germany, Switzerland and France has given him an international perspective and a scale of critical evaluations that are immeasurably worth while. He knows the best literature of all countries, for he has been an assiduous reader as well as a writer. It is to be expected that one of his prime favorites is Dostoevski, for what Jew is there who has not grown in intellectual stature under the shadow of this tremendous Russian? Bringing Asch into close touch with the various countries is the fact that many of his books have been translated into Russian and German and French. Shortly before the war he came to America, and during the past five or six years he has grown to love the United States. His work has taken on a new color from his contemporary atmosphere, and his novel, " Uncle Moses," is a direct result of his observations of the Jew in this country, and in New York in particular. Living on Staten Island with his wife and children, he is somewhat removed from the hurly-burly of the metropolis, but his work for the *Forward,* in which paper most of his novels are serialized, brings him almost daily into those literary circles of the lower East Side.

It is, perhaps, of interest briefly to point out his more important works in Yiddish, and then turn to those translations that give us an exceptionally definite idea of the merits of Asch. He has told me that he desired most strongly to have " Mary," a novel written in 1910, translated because he considered it his biggest work. But the action of " Mary " is not laid in America, and his publisher considered that " Uncle Moses," with its entire scene in New York, would prove more acceptable to English readers. " Mary " is the story of the movements and activities of the young Jews in Russia during the Revolutionary period starting in 1905. Asch has tried to crystallize in this book the aspirations of the young progressive Jew and to define clearly his prominent place in revolutionary propaganda.

Two novels by Asch which are of extreme interest are based upon the historical battles of the Jews for their faith. This is a subject upon which Asch never fails to grow enthusiastic, and it is natural that he should turn to Jewish history for documents upon which to work and express his inner feelings. One of these books, " The Sacrifice for His Holy Name," was written in direct emulation of other writers.

147

The action takes place in about 1650 and principally in Poland. Asch had in mind while he wrote the work of Nicholas Gogol, the Russian writer, and Henryk Sienkiewicz, the Pole. Gogol had given the side of the Cossacks during the religious and national upheavals of the seventeenth century in Central Europe in his " Taras Bulba." Sienkiewicz, in his trilogy, " With Fire and Sword," " The Deluge," and " Pan Michael," had done the same thing for the Poles. It was Asch's idea to write the Jewish side of this period: " The Sacrifice for His Holy Name " is the result.

The other historical novel, which was published serially in the *Forward,* is called " The Witch of Castile." The scene is laid during the papacy of Paul the Fourth in Rome, and depicts the fight of the Jews for their religion under that pitiless ruler. Asch has tried to give a minute picture of the Renaissance Ghetto of the Jews in Rome, probably the first great Ghetto that the Jews ever established. It is a surprising fact, by the way, that this Ghetto formed by Paul the Fourth in the sixteenth century was abolished only with the triumph of King Victor Emmanuel in 1870.

Two plays by Asch, untranslated as yet, may be mentioned before his more available works are treated. One of these, " The Dance of Death," is based directly upon the Great War in Europe. Another play is based upon a Biblical theme, and is called " The Two Children." The story is that of Amnon and Tamar, the children of David, and of their incestuous love for each other. It may be found in the Second Book of Kings, chapter thirteen. The theme is hardly one that could be produced in an English-speaking theatre; but those who have read it in the original are unanimous in declaring it an exceptional delicate and beautiful piece of work.

If we except a number of sketches, several one-act plays of which " Night " is the most prominent, a book of essays called "America," now out of print and difficult to procure, the fame of Sholom Asch can manifest itself to English readers only through two novels and a single play. Both of these novels are distinguished in quality, although they possess flaws, and the play was sufficiently important to achieve production by Reinhardt in his Berlin theatre.

The first novel by Sholom Asch to be translated into English was " Mottke, the Vagabond," which was brought out a number of years ago. " Gonef," the word from which " Vagabond " is fashioned in the title, literally means a gangster. Mottke is the child of misfortune, a thief who runs wild from his earliest youth, is terribly beaten and abused, and becomes the natural enemy of those in authority. The first six chapters of the book, describing the early boyhood of Mottke, are superbly written; and the character under clever handling shapes itself consistently and in high literary fashion for the reader. After that the book, which was written as a serial, grows erratic and almost picaresque in quality. Mottke runs away with a traveling troupe of entertainers who develop him into a wrestler. He continues his thieving proclivities, has a love affair with a half-wild creature who is a tight-rope walker with the troupe, and eventually murders her lover. Arriving in Warsaw, Mottke mingles with the dregs of society. The book becomes a horrible description of the very lowest forms of life. But, strangely enough, it holds the reader, for flashing through the sordidness and emphatic insistence upon gross reality are frequent bursts of beauty, lyrical interludes that remain in the memory. One feels that Mottke is the victim of adverse circumstances. He is a primitive creature, swayed by passions, and wholly oblivious to the endless shibboleths of civilized communities; at the same time, fate is always against him. He is a criminal, but he is a dreamer

150

as well. The vivid qualities of this novel have undoubtedly been strengthened by the careful study of underground Warsaw and life among the poorer classes of Jews in Poland. It is a painful book, but it is a sincere book, also.

"Uncle Moses," written but a few years ago, is in quite another vein. There is sordidness here of a sort, but there is no degeneracy. The idea that occasioned the book, according to Asch, was a true happening. Uncle Moses is a Polish Jew who comes to America, eventually establishes a sweatshop in the Bowery, and then sends back to his native village for workers. At home he was but a poor hanger-on; in America he is a power to be reckoned with. Small group by small group, he brings over the people of his native village, and it is not long before he has practically all of them, mayor, merchant, and miller, at work in his unsanitary slave-driven shop. Although he is well in his maturity and involved in affairs with various women, he violently desires the daughter of one of his workers. The girl, almost a child, is forced into marriage by avaricious parents who see in the union an easy living for themselves. Then follows a remarkable psychological exposition of the degeneration of Uncle Moses from the once proud sweatshop owner

151

to a vagabond. Almost pitiful in his attempts to win the affection of the woman he married against her will, Uncle Moses forsakes his business, his assistant cleverly steals it, and the mark of fate is set on the perplexed man. Asch has done an exceptionally fine piece of work in this novel. His characterizations are the result of more than meticulous observation. He breathes souls, sometimes tormented, into them. And the book, as a whole, becomes a valuable picture of certain aspects of Jewish life in New York.

"The God of Vengeance," Asch's one full-length play to be translated, was revived a short time ago at the Jewish Art Theatre in New York, and later was the subject of court litigation as a result of its production in English at a Broadway theatre. Its theme is such as only a continental writer could handle. The reader is given the spectacle of a man bringing up his daughter in dewy innocence and having a Holy Scroll carefully copied out for her while he runs a brothel in the cellar beneath his house. One must understand a bit of the Jewish religion to perceive the importance of the Holy Scroll. This document is the first five books of the Old Testament, beginning with Genesis, carefully written out by a scribe on vellum. Such a task some-

152

times takes years and costs an immense amount of money. It is almost as important an achievement to a religious Jew as a pilgrimage to Mecca is to a Mohammedan. The Holy Scroll, when completed, is given to a synagogue in the name of someone. In the case of " The God of Vengeance," this scroll is to be presented in the name of the daughter. The girl, however, gets downstairs to the brothel before the presentation, and the sins of the father are visited upon the head of the child. Vengeance is directed at the maddened brothel keeper through the destruction of the child's innocence. The play is tragic in quality, and over it hover the dark wings of impending fate.

These three books are sufficient to intimate rather well the qualities of Sholom Asch as a writer. The Jewish religion is an overwhelming part of his inspiration always. It is because he writes so well about Jews and knows their hearts so clearly, their famished desires and indestructible dreams, that he has become so important to them in any consideration of their contemporary literature. He is untamed at moments in a literary way, and sometimes loses that fine restraint that is so much a part of authentic achievement; but he is indubitably a born story teller, the chief requisite of a Jewish writer if he is to be popular among his own people.

In the prime of life as he is, a vast field stretches before him. The fact that already three of his books have been translated into English would seem to show that he is to emerge from that world of letters bounded by Second Avenue and stretching eastward that is so content with its own language and its own achievement. The Jew in English letters is far from a rarity, but the Jew as a writer among his own people is a thing of which we are altogether too ignorant. It is time to point out that a fully matured literature has sprung up within forty years, that it consists of remarkable novels, exceptional plays, acute spiritual and literary diagnoses, and beautiful poetry. And it may be apropos to observe that Sholom Asch is read all over the world and that it is time for him to be discovered by the country in which he lives.

DOSTOEVSKI

DOSTOEVSKI

FYODOR DOSTOEVSKI was the prophet of pain. He, more than any other writer who has ever lived, brought to the minds of the world the terrible vicissitudes of life. Out of the cerebral torture of his unhappy life, an existence overshadowed by debt and misunderstanding, he created those figures, mystics, victims of hallucination, creatures of hysteria, epileptics, idiots, moral degenerates, that people his painfully written books. In some of these figures the man himself is to be observed. Raskolnikoff in "Crime and Punishment," Myshkin in "The Idiot," even Ivan Karamazov in " The Brothers Karamazov," all have parts of the torn spiritual unrest that was an integral part of Fyodor Dostoevski's nature. It must be remembered that Dostoevski himself in his youth suffered from hallucinations and, after his release from imprisonment in Siberia, attacks of epilepsy. It was the great and distorted brain of a man who at times was almost a religious fanatic that functioned in Dostoevski.

From a certain standpoint the writer may be regarded as a Slavic exemplification of the Puritan spirit.   And this in spite of the ferocious license of some of his work.   That terrible spirit of Puritanism that made Cromwell's Roundheads so uncompromising and deliberate had touched Dostoevski, albeit it was tempered by a hysteria that was partly national and partly pathological.   He was a man of intense contradictions, and time and again he absolutely reverses certain views in his novels.   But this was because he was so essentially emotional, flung hither and thither by his passion, ceaselessly gnawing his own heart.   Evgenii Soloviev, the Russian critic, has declared that Dostoevski had a grudge against life, and this may be so, but quite often it seems that the great Russian novelist was obsessed by the conviction that life had a monstrous grudge against humanity which it paid off continually without mercy.

Like the Puritans, he hated epicureanism in all its forms.   He based himself on an iron Christian dogma that was relentless in its insistence on the moral idea.   In the figure of Raskolnikoff he presents an intellectual type, a creature of pride and individuality, only to tear it to pieces.   Raskolnikoff represented what he hated, a Nietzschean ideal that was far removed from that Christian brotherhood which he held was to save the world.   Therefore Raskolnikoff is presented only to be destroyed.   Although, after the murder, he justifies himself for the act because of his hunger and poverty, shaping his theories to exculpate himself, the inevitable judgment of Dostoevski's Puritan God makes itself manifest. In one magnificent scene in the book, that where Raskolnikoff humbly kisses the feet of the outcast Sonya in token of suffering humanity, we have the sublime theory of Dostoevski in a flash. Raskolnikoff may only find pardon when he has learned the duties of humble love and the brotherhood of man. It is toward the Christlike that man must travel.

The same thought is to be found in " The Idiot." Prince Myshkin, subject to epileptic attacks, is washed clean by his idiocy. His ignobler thoughts and moods are cleared away and it is a supremely ideal figure, suggestive of moments of Christ, that Dostoevski presents. Yet Myshkin is as incapable of good as he is of evil, in a last analysis. And here the Russian character makes its appearance. The Hamlet-like aspect of the Russian thinker is only too well known by readers of the great Russian writers. An indecision that causes them intense spiritual suffering retards them from those dynamic ends that all their thoughts would seem to lead them toward. They are contradictions, just as Dostoevski was a

159

contradiction, and just as much as Tolstoy's life was a contradiction. Cerebral victims, intellectual faineants, prophets to whose feet the mud of mutability indelibly clings, they pass through life, blindly plucking at the robe of Christ, everlastingly stumbling.

It is impossible to do more than point at Dostoevski's novels, for it is in the involved cerebral processes of their genesis, the analytical vigor and intensity of insight, that their value lies. In " Poor Folk," " The Idiot," " Crime and Punishment," " The House of the Dead," " The Brothers Karamazov," and "A Raw Youth " (a better title would be " The Hobbledehoy") the man is to be found, and it is from those pages only that a proper perspective of Fyodor Dostoevski may be reached. These studies of morbid, diseased, criminal minds cannot be adequately presented in any critical analysis. Dostoevski himself has done all the analysis in his books.

Concerned so with the submerged stratas of Russian life, one would think that Dostoevski's urge would be toward the Russian peasant, but that is not so. The Russian writer was essentially a child of the city. It is the night scenes of Petrograd, suffering people in wretched hovels with the snow rushing down outside, that is ever in his mind. Here in the turmoil and dirt and madness of the city he finds his characters, writing into them his own religious moods, leading them in the straight ways of suffering. His characters, extraordinarily fine at certain moments, are never completely rounded and fulfilled to their extreme possibilities. Life was a struggle for Dostoevski, and he had no time to polish his work to that literary excellency attained by Turgenev, for instance. Even from the same reason he expended no care on the development of his women characters. One would be hard put to it to find a fully presented lovely woman in any of his tales. The mood for it simply did not come to him. He was more concerned with blows than caresses. Love, when it does appear in his books, is generally a torture. Romance was alien to him, and the affecting scenes that star the work of certain other Russian writers are not to be found in Dostoevski's books. It is the same with descriptions of nature. Dostoevski, mightily concerned with the tattered passions of the human soul in its struggles against injustice, had no time to paint pictures of nature. They are implicit in his work at times, but never developed. The vivid qualities of his description are rather to be found in those chapters treating the underlife of Petrograd.

Yet this man, this Great Epileptic of God, has laid a mighty hand on Russian letters that time will hardly displace. He was a phenomenon, a dæmonic dreamer who brought a strange, tortured magic into beauty and love and life long before Nietszche or Maeterlinck. There is about his characters at times a mysticism that suggests certain subtle overtones. It was a vast pity that welled in Dostoevski, and it was so vast that it unbalanced his mind, distorted his perspectives, and sometimes changed through a most consistent process of unfulfillment into sheer savagery. Who can doubt this love holding out both hands to life only to have life make the great abnegation? Who can doubt the torture and unrest of the man at the abrupt realization of the incongruous malevolence of life?

The man himself was bitter. He had more right to the name "Gorki" than Aleksei Pyeshkov. Partly owing to his hysterical temperament, he deliberately made himself at odds with many of the writers of his day. Early quarrels with Bielinsky and Nekrasof might be expected, for the natures of these men held nothing in common with the young Dostoevski, who looked to them for his means of livelihood. He had become acquainted with the bony hand of poverty under his own father, a staff physician who supported his family on a mere pittance, and all his life this spectre was to pursue him. After his first brief success in Petrograd in artistic circles, he found many of the writers of his day antagonistic to him. They loved to bait the excitable, high-strung writer, inveigle him into arguments, until Dostoevski lost his temper and declared the most outrageous things. Turgenev was one of those writers who loved to bait Dostoevski, and Turgenev was hated all his life by the young writer. At first there appeared the possibility that they would be friends. We find the twenty-four-year-old writer stating in a letter to his brother Michael: " Bielinsky declares that Turgenev has quite lost his heart to me. T. is really a splendid person! I've almost lost my own heart to him." But this mood was not to last. Dostoevski, always sincere in what he wrote, could not sympathize with the writings of Turgenev, and Turgenev found nothing in common with the younger man.

The story of the quarrel which took place in 1867 is to be found in a letter from Dostoevski to Apollon Maikov. " I can't understand the aristocratic and pharisaical sort of way he embraces one, and offers his cheek to be kissed," rages Dostoevski in his long letter. According to Dostoevski, he found Turgenev in an irritable mood over the failure of "Smoke." After declaring that he could not have imagined anybody so clumsily displaying the wounds to his vanity, Dostoevski flies into a rage at Turgenev's statement that he was an uncompromising atheist. The fanatical religious spirit of Dostoevski manifests itself here as it did all through his life. Nihilism was anathema to Dostoevski, although he had suffered imprisonment in Siberia for revolutionary utterances. Turgenev appears to have adopted a Prussian attitude during this visit. He declared that Russia was bound to crawl in the dust before Germany and that he was writing a long article against the Russophiles and Slavophiles. Dostoevski advised him to secure a telescope from Paris for his better convenience. "What do you mean?" asked Turgenev. We may imagine his choler beginning to rise. "The distance is somewhat great," replied Dostoevski. "Direct the telescope on Russia, and then you will be able to observe us; otherwise you really can't see anything at all." "He flew into a rage," adds Dostoevski. "When I saw him so angry, I said with well-simulated naivete: 'Really I should never have supposed that all the articles derogatory to your new novel could have discomposed you to this extent. By God, the thing's not worth getting so angry about. Come, spit upon it all!' " Turgenev's answer was: " I'm not in the least discomposed. What are you thinking of?" How red with indignation Turgenev must have been by this time! Dostoevski was so obviously sneering at him that a quarrel was inevitable. Upon Dostoevski finishing a tirade against Germany and Germans, Turgenev found his opportunity to explode. "In speaking thus, you insult me personally," he cried. " You know quite well that I have definitely settled here, that I consider myself a German and not a Russian, and am proud of it." There were a few more words and the two men parted. Turgenev cut Dostoevski several weeks later when they accidentally met in a railway station.

There is no use attempting to analyze this hatred between the two finest Russian writers of their day. Dostoevski was undoubtedly a man who hated strongly and made no attempts to hide it. Time and again in his letters he showed that he lacked the power of controlling himself. His ideas on life and letters were definite. And it is a fact that quite often he muddled up the man and his work, judging one from the other. If he did not like a book, it was quite possible that he would not like the author either.

Just what Dostoevski brought to the Russian people is a question that is argued even today. That, in great measure, he wakened an interest in the masses, bringing Russian intellectualism closer to the lower classes, cannot be doubted. Dostoevski's attitude is largely based upon an intense sympathy for the squalid, perverse, criminal masses. Without the people he knew that there could be no authentic progress, and the condition of the people he blamed upon the tyrannical cruelty of environment and social conditions. If we put aside certain Chauvinistic views which he expressed only occasionally, we shall find that Dostoevski's ethical views were based pretty closely upon the Sermon on the Mount. This attitude is undoubtedly obscured at times by the neurotic tendencies of the man. He was an intensive liberator in a way. " True freedom," he declared, " is such an overcoming of the will that at length one may attain to a moral condition wherein one shall always, and under every circumstance, and in very deed and truth, possess the mastery over one's self." This is a long step from the individualism that later made itself evident in Russia, the Sanine cult of Michael Artzibashev, for instance. It was the old Holy Russian attitude, the Christlike gesture of selflessness that Tolstoy was to attempt to put into practice years later. A return to the people, what Evgenii Soloviev calls " service of the masses in a spirit of Christian love and truth," was Dostoevski's message to his people. What Russia has made of that message is evident today. Dostoevski's centenary (Oct. 30, 1921) found the country he loved so passionately and for which he passed through such spiritual suffering a spectacle before which we may be very sure the great writer would bow his weary head in hopelessness.

HARDY AND HOUSMAN

HARDY AND HOUSMAN

HE kinship between Thomas Hardy and A. E. Housman is manifest not so much in certain objective treatments of their poetic material as in a deeper consciousness of the dark and serious business of life shared by both of them. The ironic note, developed more fully in the work of Hardy, is fainter in the poems of Housman; indeed, it is difficult to draw the line between the latter poet's pessimism and his ironic acceptance of certain facts. His nature is not so robust as that of Hardy. The note is thinner; he approaches death in a sadly contemplative mood:

> In the nation that is not
>   Nothing stands that stood before:
> There revenges are forgot,
>   And the hater hates no more;
> Lovers lying two and two
>   Ask not who they sleep beside
> And the bridegroom all night through
>   Never turns him to the bride.

It is the regret of life, a recognizance of the pathetic fallacy of death, that stirs Housman so poignantly. He sighs for rose-lipped maidens and light-foot lads. The deplorable madness of war and its romantic clutch upon youth arouse him to those carefully combed stanzas that become so impressive almost because of their simplicity. Regret, the nostalgia for passing things, stirs sadly behind the verses. Paraphrasing a French poet, he'll to the woods no more—

> The laurels all are cut,
> The bowers are bare of May
> That once the Muses wore.

But Hardy is different. He, too, regards with evident pain the futility of existence beneath the shadow of an unknown thing. Life, however, does not call to him so tearfully as it does to Housman. His irony is his armor, and, though at times his laughter becomes discordant and cruel, it always saves him from lachrymose attitudes. He can say:

I never cared for Life: Life cared for me,
And hence I owe it some fidelity.
It now says, " Cease; at length thou hast learnt to grind
Sufficient toll for an unwilling mind,
And I dismiss thee—not without regard
That thou didst ask no ill-advised reward,
Nor sought in me much more than thou couldst find."

Those lines are headed " Epitaph " in Mr. Hardy's latest, and possibly his last, book of poems, " Late Lyrics and Earlier." Coming, as this book did, simultaneously with " Last Poems " by A. E.

172

Housman, manifestly that author's final work in poetry, it offers an unusual opportunity for comparison. Both men move in a great tradition. Both of them were rebels to that tradition. Both turned their backs upon the mellifluous Victorianism that witnessed their approach to maturity. They adjusted their visions to a brave observation of life as it really was with the romantic veils torn away. In a certain sense, both of them were realists. But I am inclined to believe that the spiritual disturbance over life and its mystery is more emphatic in the work of Thomas Hardy than it is in that of Housman. Hardy believed in a cold acceptance of actualities, but this was far from pessimism, for he never wholly despairs over existence. He declared in a poem, " If way to the Better there be, it exacts a full look at the Worst," and it is because he stares so fixedly at the Worst that we denominate him a pessimist. As he himself remarks, his mind is concerned with " evolutionary meliorism." He believes that if we know the Worst we may in some measure ameliorate it. At the same time he always reserves the right to doubt, and he frankly speaks of " the modicum of free will conjecturally possessed by organic life." There is an ironic note here, and throughout practically the entire bulk of his work (except when he is merely farcical) this irony may be observed. Indeed, the very nature of the man is ironic. Still, irony is on a higher plane than pessimism. Anybody can be pessimistic; it takes a genius to be actually ironic.

At the same time pessimism may be translated into a beautiful and lyrical mood, and this is what Housman does. His clean, incisive stanzas are weighted with an undemonstrative beauty, and if this beauty at times becomes the dark shadow of ominous wings it is none the less a beauty that holds the heart and raises a lump in the throat. All beauty is sad; it is as sad in the work of Hardy as it is in that of Housman. But behind the beauty in Hardy's verses functions the inevitable brain; it is more cerebral, more dominated by a conscious prodding of inquiring will. This is not so with Housman. His thought is rich, but it never rises beyond a sad hazard at things. He is gravely lyrical, and this is one of his prime beauties. Hardy, on the other hand, delivers himself of a broken melody. It is not spontaneous; the reader feels a profound intelligence doggedly tearing its way toward a musical utterance. But that utterance, once reached, haunts the reader as much as do the felicitously turned verses of Housman.

The inevitable comparison between "Last Poems" and "A Shropshire Lad" must be made, and it can hardly pain Housman to realize that the last book is no better than the volume which preceded it by twenty-six years. Housman, the poet, existed in the 1890s, and "Last Poems" is but a gift flung forward from that time. This later book may be regarded as an addition, a forgotten annex, to the first. Nothing in it is quite as fine as the best utterances in "A Shropshire Lad," but for all of that it is cut from the same cloth. Indeed, the mood is amazingly the same as that in the older book. One reason for this, of course, is the fact that many of these poems which have but recently been published were written back in the early days of "A Shropshire Lad." How well this small piece would have fitted in the former volume:

> Oh stay at home, my lad, and plough
> The land and not the sea,
> And leave the soldiers at their drill,
> And all about the idle hill
> Shepherd your sheep with me.
> Oh stay with company and mirth
> And daylight and the air;
> Too full already is the grave
> Of fellows that were good and brave
> And died because they were.

175

Like many of Housman's poems, these words fall lightly on the ear, and it is not until one stops to think about them that the perfection of phrasing and quiet poignancy of thought in the last three lines begin to manifest their magic. This subdued art, this mastering of a form until it reaches the high beauty of simplicity, this handling of ordinary words in a manner to transform them, is part of the secret of Housman's poetry. How easy it is to remember phrases from " A Shropshire Lad," such as " Runners whom renown outran and the name died before the man," or " By brooks too broad for leaping the lightfoot lads are laid," in which nothing but the simplest words are used, and yet they are strung together with such a pale high tenderness that the heart almost stops at their poignancy. The same is true of " Last Poems," although to a lesser degree. The tone of the first book—part of it a deep pity for mankind—is carried on. At times, although seldom, a brighter color, a more Oriental imagination, starts from the pearl-gray shadowy woof of the book. Such a brief flare of color may be found in these lines, for instance:

> West and away the wheels of darkness roll,
>   Day's beamy banner up the east is borne,
> Spectres and fears, the nightmare and her foal,
>   Drown in the golden deluge of the morn.

But over sea and continent from sight
  Safe to the Indies has the earth conveyed
The vast and moon-eclipsing cone of night,
  Her towering foolscap of eternal shade.

See, in mid-heaven the sun is mounted; hark,
  The belfries tingle to the noonday chime.
'Tis silent, and the subterranean dark
  Has crossed the nadir, and begins to climb.

No one can deny the imagination exemplified in the last two lines of the second stanza of this poem. But it is not often that Housman goes out of his way to perfect such phrasing. Rather does his magic depend on the unexpected turn of the simple phrase.

The " lightfoot " Shropshire lads that move through the poetry of Housman travel always in the Valley of the Shadow of Death. The grim specter looms ever at their sides, ready to trip them up in the race, to scream at them from the rushing bullet, to lay them low when brains and eyes are at their brightest. Turning to the poetry of Thomas Hardy, we find that his Wessex lads also pass through a dark valley, but it is not so much that of death as of disillusionment. There is more characterization in Hardy's work. Stories are told; anecdotes are presented; individuals are painted. In

177

" Late Lyrics and Earlier " the reader will discover
a wealth of poetry and, perhaps, Hardy at his very
finest as a poet. This is not so amazing when we
recollect that these poems do not represent merely
the closing years of a rich life, but are collected from
all periods of that existence. The closing poems are
there, poems that indicate that Hardy has reached
the final stage of his development. How tenderly
and yet how whimsically he acknowledges the young
and fiery bloods that would thrust him into the limbo
of out-moded things! His special message for them
may be found in " An Ancient to Ancients," in which
he says :

> We who met sunrise sanguine-souled,
>   Gentlemen,
> Are wearing weary. We are old;
> These younger press; we feel our rout
> Is imminent to Aides' den, —-
> The evening's shades are stretching out,
>   Gentlemen!
>
> And yet, though ours be failing frames,
>   Gentlemen,
> So were some others' history names,
> Who trod their track light-limbed and fast
> As these youth, and not alien
> From enterprise, to their long last,
>   Gentlemen.

Sophocles, Plato, Socrates,
        Gentlemen,
Pythagoras, Thucydides,
Herodotus, and Homer, — yea,
Clement, Augustin, Origen,
Burnt brightlier towards their setting day,
        Gentlemen.

And ye, red-lipped and smoothbrowed, list,
        Gentlemen;
Much is there waits you we have missed;
Much lore we leave you worth the knowing,
Much, much has lain outside our ken:
Nay, rush not; time serves: we are going,
        Gentlemen.

Although the bower shrined to Tennyson is roof-wrecked and she for whom the rhymes were written is dust, no one can observe the departure of this Ancient without a catch at the throat. He dominates an entire period of letters, although it has been evident in poetry but of recent years. He, the creator of Tess, of Jude, of Bathsheba, of Henchard, about to depart? One gazes about at the younger men and wonders who will ever occupy that lofty seat.

"Late Lyrics and Earlier" contains all those peculiar ingredients that have already made Hardy's poetry so individual. There is the same ironical twist to stories that otherwise would merely be

179

macabre.   Death dances through the mazes of life's
flutterings.   With an acrid penetration the poet
pierces the mask of things and touches the white
bone behind.   And running always side by side with
his love of character portrayal and philosophical expression is that love of nature, of flowers and wet
fields and soil.   He is essentially a tragedian, but
he is an ironic tragedian.   Housman, on the other
hand, must be termed a romantic and lyrical tragedian.   A sharp analysis of Hardy's last book would,
I think, show that his virtues have been transcended
and his faults have been minimized.   In other words,
he is in sure control of his instrument, and " Late
Lyrics and Earlier" becomes his best book of poems.
An example from this book of Hardy at his best,
telling a poignant tale and illuminating it with the
last four beautiful lines, may be found in this poem
called " The Whitewashed Wall:"

> Why does she turn in that shy soft way
>   Whenever she stirs the fire,
> And kiss to the chimney-corner wall,
>   As if entranced to admire
> Its whitewashed bareness more than the sight
>   Of a rose in richest green?
> I have known her long, but this raptured rite
>   I never before have seen.

—Well, once when her son cast his shadow there,
  A friend took a pencil and drew him
Upon that flame-lit wall. And the lines
  Had a lifelike semblance to him.
And there long stayed his familiar look;
  But one day, ere she knew,
The whitener came to cleanse the nook,
  And covered the face from view.

" Yes," he said: "My brush goes on with a rush,
  And the draught is buried under;
When you have to whiten old cots and brighten,
  What else can you do, I wonder?"
But she know's he's there. And when she yearns
  For him, deep in the laboring night,
She sees him as close at hand, and turns
  To him under his sheet of white.

The secret of great poetry, beyond all analysis,
is in these verses. The verses are simple enough
and so is the phrasing, yet something transforms
them into a magic that is Hardy's own.   Other
pieces give the same effect; for instance, there is the
poem called " On a Discovered Curl of Hair," or,
as another example, " A Woman Driving."   The
book, as a whole, is essentially somber; more so,
perhaps, than those which have preceded it; but it
is a high somberness, a quality removed far above
mere pessimism. The personality which it displays

is one that is always attuned to the delicate hints and advances of beauty, although the stark note at times reaches the majesty of ancient Greek utterance.

Two statements, one from each book, should call forth dismay in the minds of poetry lovers. Mr. Housman declares, " It is not likely that I shall ever be impelled to write much more," and Mr. Hardy writes, " I believe that those readers who care for my poems at all—readers to whom no passport is required—will care for this new installment of them, perhaps the last, as much as for any that have preceded them." Both men imply that their last books lie before their readers. For men (and women) who came to maturity in the late nineties there is something in these statements that hurts. One can but think sadly of the last four lines in Mr. Housman's book:

> To-morrow, more's the pity,
>   Away we both must hie,
> To air the ditty,
>   And to earth I.

At least they go trailing clouds of glory, and, though they walked in shadowy ways, there is something in their aristocratic indomitability of purpose that must flare as a beacon for generations of younger writers.

182

They were true to their art, and their accomplishment has been of single issue—an uncompromising achievement of beauty as they saw it. And though they doubted—the gods should be good to them.

GEORGIAN FICTION

GEORGIAN FICTION

RUPERT BROOKE, whose singing days were ended by the burning sun off Scyros, welcomed war and the chance that it afforded young men

> To turn, as swimmers into cleanness leaping,
> Glad from a world grown old and cold and weary,
> Leave the sick hearts that honor could not move,
> And half-men, and their dirty songs and dreary,
> And all the little emptiness of love.

It was a state of mind that had obvious reasons for its being; indeed, it was a logical development from the breakdown of Victorian sentimentalism through the weary and often neurotic gasp of the Yellow Nineties to the subjective realism of what we designate as the Georgian era. Nowhere is this changed spirit more evident than in contemporary English fiction, and particularly is it crystallized in the short-story form, a form that has resolved itself into a series of pathological investigations, at least in the work of many representative figures. Whether or not this is good for literature is not the question; it is assuredly logical, a natural culmination of certain trends that could end in no other way.

187

Two paramount reasons would seem to exist for this modern type of fiction. One is an intense disillusionment that has saved itself from utter despair by an abrupt cynicism. The other is an undiverted urge for subjective rendition, for realistic analyses and a defiant abnegation of sentimentality in all its forms. The disillusionment has come about through the crashing down of the old scaffolding upon which were reared those ideals that we call Victorian. If we turn back to Dickens, Lytton, Trollope, Mrs. Gaskell, Miss Mulock and their contemporaries we will find a forced sentimentalism, an emphatic coating of unpleasant truths with the rosy-tinted plaster of romance. It is only in certain aspects of Thackeray that we observe prefiguring of that cynicism that was to grow so greatly in the years that followed, that expressed itself as wistful melancholy, as romantic pessimism, as lyrical mysticism in the 1890s and only later became the unveiled realistic weighing of values that we have today. The young writers, having turned their backs on the old traditional expression, found facing them a bleak expanse that needed to be explored with new methods. Then came the subjective investigation, the psychoanalytic study, the starkly unsentimental presentations of life. Intellectual England became blasé, coldly sophisticated, and this is what we feel throughout most of " Georgian Stories: 1922," a book peculiarly adapted to be a text for a sermon on the contemporary English scene as it is exemplified in fiction. Even in those tales that do not end tragically we find a sophisticated flirting with realistic values. There is nothing that approaches sentimentality in the true sense. Many a situation that of old would have lended itself to a sentimental rendition has been twisted to a mocking conclusion.

Twenty-two writers contribute to " Georgian Stories: 1922," a book obviously compiled as a companion-volume to the admirable series of " Georgian Poetry " that has been appearing for some years now. These writers exemplify much more forcefully than mere argument could do the rather kindred trends in modern English fiction. If one chooses to affirm that the writers of a period express the spirit of that period, then it must be energetically maintained that contemporary England is intensely cerebral, tragically inclined, cynically sophisticated, blasé, and, on the whole, rather world-weary. Ten of the writers concerned in " Georgian Stories: 1922 " contribute tragedies, and these tragedies range from the mere shockers by F. Tennyson Jesse

189

and Sheila Kaye-Smith (not a good example of her work, by the way) to the deeper, more significant tragedies of the soul implicit in May Sinclair's " The Bambino " and D. H. Lawrence's " The Shadow in the Rose-Garden." It is pertinent to note that both of these last-mentioned tragedies are concerned with insanity, as is Oliver Onion's " Io." An unpleasant disillusionment of the spirit lurks in some of these tragedies, E. Somerset Maugham's " Rain," for instance, and Stacy Aumonier's " The Beautiful Merciless Lady." Just why this generation is so concerned with tragedy is not difficult to comprehend. Death has become an obsession in more ways than one and the dark frustration of the spirit that generally culminates in death is part of the disillusionment that the war brought. It is futile to assert that the war had any great influence on letters. The spirit that made the war was a spirit of disillusionment and the four years in France was not a starting point, but a natural consequence. Rupert Brooke was aware of his " world grown old and cold and weary " before the guns began and, like a number of the very young, he sought a regeneration in that fiery bath of flame and steel that did not come. The world was just as " old and cold and weary " after the armistice as it was in 1914.

190

Death, playing so large a part in the short stories in this book and holding, as it does, the minds of Stacy Aumonier, W. Somerset Maugham, F. Tennyson Jesse, Sheila Kaye-Smith, D. H. Lawrence, Lennox Robinson, Algernon Blackwood and Ethel Colburn Mayne, must be admitted as one of the obsessions of the younger group. Indeed, two of the stories, " The Coach," by Violet Hunt, and " Mr. Andrews," by E. M. Forster, are concerned with the ghosts of the already dead. A macabre supernatural quality impregnates both these stories and both of them are hopeless in their outlook. They satirize life after death and scorn the idea of heaven. Two other tales are supernatural phantasies, " Perez," by W. L. George, and " The Criminal," by J. D. Beresford, both of them being composed in a mocking spirit. Still another, apparently based on an old Irish legend, that might be termed supernatural is " A Pair of Muddy Shoes," by Lennox Robinson. The gruesome quality is also evident in Algernon Blackwood's " The Tryst " and Ethel Colburn Mayne's " Lovells Meeting," both of which concern men who love women who have suddenly died, the deaths of these women coming as blows to the men.

Turning to a different genre, tragic in its way yet not directly concerned with physical death albeit

191

the death of the spirit forms no small part, there are the disillusioned social comedies, "Speed the Plough," by Mary Butts; "The First Violin," by Norman Davey; "Pictures," by the late Katherine Mansfield, and "The Perfect Wife," by Elinor Mordaunt. Here again is another largely looming aspect of modern English fiction. This expression of disillusionment takes several forms. It may be a rounded plot- structure as in "The Perfect Wife" or it may be the incisive development of a single character as in "Pictures." One gathers from these stories that the social edifice of England as viewed by a number of the younger writers is suffering from dry-rot; the beams are sagging and about to split. Especially is this suggested in "The Perfect Wife," with its reminiscence of the famous feast of King Ahasuerus in the first part. Here we have the self-demolition of a man through his own vileness. Stacy Aumonier's "The Beautiful Merciless Lady" is also concerned with the self-destruction of a man, but it is written in a different key than "The Perfect Wife." A few shreds of romance still cling to Aumonier's pen, but Elinor Mordaunt is dauntlessly realistic.

The few comedies in the book do not rank either in pertinence or literary importance with the other

stories. " George's Gender," by Basil MacDonald
Hastings, is amusing but slight, and it handles a situation that would have been tabooed in Victorian
times with a sly insouciance that suggests "La Vie
Parisienne." Alec Waugh's " The Intruder " is a
more serious bit of sophisticated action. The situation avoids the distasteful by clever handling. One
story that does not quite fit into any category is a
daring bit of work, and this is " A Scrap of Paper,"
by Arnold Lunn. It is laid in an English boys'
school. As a study of conditions and, at the same
time, an exemplification of schoolboy loyalty, it deserves praise. Arnold Lunn is a new name as far
as American readers are concerned, but he is not
the least important figure in this book.

One thing is invariably obvious in all of these
stories, a trait that is hardly so signficant in the tales
of the Victorian era. And this is the great concern
which these modern English writers exhibit about
modern existence. In the old days a man or a woman
wrote a story because he or she had a good plot or
an amusing character to describe. It was an objective form, an observation of life from the outside
and it was exaggerated without self-consciousness
when exaggeration would seem to improve its quality
and better sustain the reader's interest. Unreality

193

might creep in, the action might creak rather badly, but if the narrative gift of the writer was sufficient these detractions did not matter. The Victorians wrote voluminously, easily, not stopping to wrack their brains too much about life and its multifarious manifestations. The modern writer is different. It is life itself that absorbs his interest and not the opportunity to make a pretty picture of life. He has certain convictions about the social scene, about its lapses, about the dry-rot that he sees creeping into it, and he fashions his stories with the idea of bringing these thoughts before his readers. It is true that some of the older writers (certainly Dickens) did this, but they did it by exaggeration. They whipped a social crime—child labor, school systems or what-not—by a determined overpainting. The moderns are more subtle. Life as it is appears in their stories; there are no sentimental veils to make it more attractive. Virtue does not always triumph. An inexorable and logical realism pervades the page and the reader must take the stark picture as it is given.

Certain questions that heretofore were not brought up in fiction appear in these modern stories. Religion, for instance, and the idea of life after death engrosses the modern writer. The real value

194

and sincerity of moral statutes is questioned. In fact, the entire edifice erected by our grandfathers is being swarmed over by countless writers who are testing the beams, peering through the windows, kicking down the pillars. The young writers take themselves with intense seriousness. This is assuredly obvious in " Georgian Stories: 1922." The problems of the universe do not daunt them and they tackle the problems that their fathers dodged with a fine cynical astuteness that carries convictions to their contemporaries at least, if it does not to their elders.

It would be hardly fair to select any two or three writers as the best in this book, for they represent too many varying facets of modern English fiction. But it should be pointed out that Katherine Mansfield's " Pictures " again emphasizes the loss to contemporary letters occasioned by her untimely death. The fine sense of sophisticated reality that was so large a part of her talent is at its best in " Pictures," a somewhat mordant study of a penniless actress who takes the easiest way. And certain names not too well known in America crop up in this volume with such pleasurable consequences that one can but wish more of them. For instance, there is Violet

Hunt. Her story, " The Coach," is possibly based on an old English bit of folk-lore, for it describes a trip of the Coach of Death, driven by a headless driver, and filled with people lately dead. The gruesome quality is there, but it is lightened by a certain whimsical touch, a sophisticated jauntiness of rendering that many of the younger writers seem to bring to the depiction of death. Death has apparently lost its terror for the young. Possibly life proved too cheap during the past decade. Still another writer of more than ordinary excellence is Ethel Colburn Mayne, whose " Lovells Meeting " is possibly the most subtle piece of work in the book. One looks for omissions from the book and relying on a rather limited knowledge of modern English short stories observes but few. Lennox Robinson, of course, is the only Irishman included; and if he is to be a Georgian author one wonders why Daniel Corkery, Brinsley MacNamara and James Joyce (whose " Dubliners " was an astounding volume of short stories) are not included. Then there is Aldous Huxley. Certainly he is a Georgian of significance and should have been included. A tale from his " Mortal Coils " would have rounded the book out, giving it a satirical finish which it rather lacks. Others who come to mind are Virginia Woolf and

196

Leonard Merrick. But possibly they do not quite enter into the spirit of the volume.

It should be pointed out that the compiler of " Georgian Stories: 1922 " is rather addicted to the morbid and this may have emphasized the impression of the contemporary atmosphere in England. But it is doubtful if this has been mistranslated to any large extent. So many names of importance abound and it is so obvious that the natural moods of these writers are expressed in the stories included that the judgment could not be seriously altered even with the inclusion of more cheerful writers. The spirit is there for all to perceive and it is indubitably one of cynical acceptance and sophisticated observation.

197

THE LETTERS OF A SHAKESPEAREAN SPECIALIST

THE LETTERS OF A SHAKESPEAREAN
SPECIALIST

HE publication of the correspondence of Horace Howard Furness rather abruptly brings home to the writer the fact that American specialists in literature are few and far between. The general critic, the broad commentator, the scholarly scribbler of marginal notes upon letters, may be found in abundance, but how difficult it is to group together more than a meager handful of men who have consecrated their lives and brains to a single gigantic undertaking. It is different in England. There one may note a dozen Shakespearean specialists, or Professor Gilbert Murray whose whole existence is inextricably interwoven with Greek drama, or Professor James Frazer who has devoted the bulk of his life to the solitary achievement of " The Golden Bough."

It takes a great enthusiasm to so subdue one's self to a single aspect of culture, for man is naturally a gregarious animal and the high power of consistent concentration is both a gift and the result of an iron will.

Mr. Furness was such a man. He had but one objective in life, and that was to so digest and parallel the great world of commentaries concerned with Shakespeare's plays as to afford all Shakespeare lovers a Variorum Edition that should be the final word in collation. In a certain measure he was a creator also, for his own personality is indubitably a part of the large volumes which now stand as a memorial to his auspicious industry. It was a rich, humorous, childlike personality, compact with sweetness and good will. The man may be found in his letters, and they but emphasize the nature that unmistakably peeps out between the more scholarly lines of his Shakespearean comment. Mr. Furness loved his gentle jokes, worshiped his friends, made it impossible for others to quarrel with him concerning a subject about which most critics violently wrangle, and passed his placid, somewhat hermit-like existence amid the rare atmosphere of the library. He was a scholar in the best sense of the word. By no means a mere pedant, yet he was almost miraculously patient in his exhaustive labors.

His life, as it is revealed in his letters, was not so much an objective matter as a subjective development of a unique temperament. There is not much that stands out as of unusual interest; perhaps the one episode of his quiet days was his work on the Seybert Commission when he investigated spiritualism in an endeavor to establish the true facts regarding the claims of mediums. It was a bizarre undertaking, but Mr. Furness proved to be peculiarly qualified. He was an investigator in the best sense of the word, for he possessed that happy faculty of unremitting research and clear analysis that is so much a part of the virtues of the Variorum Shakespeare. Born early in the nineteenth century, the son of a Unitarian clergyman, he was graduated from Harvard University in 1854, had the usual two years of travel in Europe, and then took up the study of law. The outbreak of the Civil War found him prepared to enter active service, but already that deafness which was to be his great burden during the major part of his lifetime was upon him, and he was refused by army doctors. But Mr. Furness had not offered himself as a gesture. He meant to serve, and during the greater part of the struggle he worked valiantly with the Sanitary Commission. His marriage was peculiarly happy, and, being luckily beyond the need to labor for a livelihood, he turned to the study of Shakespeare. The rest of his life is the history of the Variorum Shakespeare, fifteen plays being completed before his death in 1912.

No one dipping into the two finely printed volumes of his letters can fail to develop an affection for the man. He was so patient, even humorous, under the affliction of stone deafness. He was so bright and apt in his critical retorts, comments, and explanations to men like Wright and Rolfe. He was so mellow, so delectably old-fashioned (if the phrase may be used in its kindliest sense), so spiritually beaming. Merry and charming in his old age, it is easy and pleasant to picture him seated in his large library, painstakingly reading and digesting every scrap of important comment on Shakespeare, comparing folios and editions, noting even a displaced letter in the immortal lines of his favorite author. It was a quiet, sedentary existence, but an ideal one in many ways. It was far from the din and hullabaloo of infuriated criticism. It was scholarship in its old, aristocratic sense. In short, it was an unusual picture in the cultural life of America. Mr. Furness was the ideal type of specialist, and we may guess that he got quite as much enjoyment and profit out of his grubbing through old folios and half-forgotten commentaries as we do who run madly as we read.

So much of the man is revealed in his correspondence that no better picture of him may be obtained than by frequent excursions into it. For instance, he narrates fully in a letter to Rolfe the inception of the Variorum Shakespeare, and it may well be set down here. He wrote:

"As for the time when I began to work over Shakespeare and study him with zeal, it began in '62 or '63 when I made a mighty Variorum 'Hamlet,' cutting out the notes of five or six editions, besides the Variorum of 1821, and pasting them on a page with a little rivulet of text. 'Twas a ponderous book, of Qto. size and eight or nine inches thick — I took great delight in burning it some years ago. But the work revealed to me that it was high time to begin a new Variorum, that we might start afresh. We are constantly threshing old straw. In ' Romeo and Juliet,' you remember, I added after each note the editors who had adopted it, with or without credit to the old Variorum. But I dropped the plan in the next volume. 'Twas open to many objections. I chose ' Rom. and Jul.' as the first, merely because I was enamoured with the play and I thought 'twas probable that I should never edit a second. Lippincott agreed to print it because he wanted to make a show at the Vienna Exposition and get the prize for a perfect book, which he did I think I tried five or six different shapes, sizes and styles before I settled down on the present one, with varying faced type. To avoid the imputation that I was self-seeking in attaching my puny name to ' the greatest in all literature,' I resolved that I would be the merest drudge, simply arranging and codifying the notes of others and would utter no faintest chirp of my own. But, as you know, my resolution did not hold out, and now, ever since I edited ' Othello,' I gabble like a tinker. Dear me! how old I am! Dyce and Harness died when ' R. and J.' was going through the press. But I had most kind notes of encouragement from Charles Knight and Keightly, and with Collier and Staunton I corresponded on most familiar terms for years — so also Halliwell. As for Aldis Wright — brothers cannot be on more cordial terms than he and I, and yet our acquaintance began in storms and wrath in the pages of the 'Athenæum.' He and I are the only survivors of that old group. By touching hands with Collier, I reach back through Malone to Steevens, to Dr. Johnson, to Capell, to Theobald, and to Pope. ' I feel chilly and grown old.' "

This extremely illuminating letter was written in 1900, and it orientates the position of Mr. Furness in Shakespearean letters better than any page of description could. The commentator's modesty is evident throughout. Indeed, this is one of the most prominent traits revealed by Mr. Furness in his letters. He was always deprecatory about his own importance. " I am not really a lion, but only Bottom the weaver," he asserts to Rolfe. But he underestimated himself. He was important, and he did do something for which there was a crying need, and he did it with surprising excellence. Conservative he was, but his conservatism did not materially lessen his importance as a co-ordinator of Shakespearean criticism. He was always open-minded, and nowhere is it evident that he ever twisted or perverted a judgment or illumination of Shakespeare's genius because he personally did not approve of the conclusions.

Mr. Furness was sweet-minded in the most idealistic sense, and, blessedly enough, he labored before psychoanalysis became the scalpel of criticism. He took his Shakespeare at face value and did not try to read hidden morbidities into obviously innocent lines. It is safe to assert that he would have taken small joy in Frank Harris's theories about the Swan of Avon. It must not be imagined that Mr. Furness was in any sense of the word gullible. He was far from that. His logic is undeniable and his assiduity at reaching proper conclusions inexhaustible. We have evidence of this in the notes to " Othello," for instance, where he dilates on the medical aspects of Desdemona's death, getting the opinions of no less than seven or eight physicians, among them S. Weir Mitchell, before he is through with the topic. He wants the thing right. He wants to point out Shakespeare's mistakes where they exist, but he does not want to impinge his own groundless theories on the poet's work and then twist the great lines to his own conjectures.

The importance of Mr. Furness's contributions to Shakespearean criticism must be arrived at by greater scholars than the writer of this article, but even a general reader must observe their lucidity and reasonableness. Of course the primary function of the Variorum Shakespeare is far from an outlet for Mr. Furness's opinions. It is shaped to carry in parallel form the conclusions of all the great Shakespearean scholars, and this function is beautifully fulfilled. The books are large books, but they are large in many ways besides mere bulk. Mr. Furness arrived at his own opinions by careful study of the text, and he held to them in spite of adverse criticism. For instance, he scouted the theory that Hamlet was mad in his preface to the Variorum " Hamlet," and of course brought down upon his head a clattering of verbal brickbats. Writing to Francis J. Child just before the appearance of the " Hamlet," he jovially remarks:

" I am heartily glad that you scout Hamlet's insanity. The insanity is in the critics; only tell it not to Gath and let it not be known in Askelon that this is my opinion. I'm afraid if it were known, I couldn't go within a league of an Insane Asylum without being caught and clapped in a strait waist-coat. As you say, we are all of us insane in one sense of the word; that is, all of us sensible fellows, and very thankful to God we ought to be for it too."

And in a later letter he remarks:

" Critics are falling foul of me in all directions for saying in my Preface to Hamlet that the Dan-ish Prince was neither mad nor pretended to be so. Though I have reasons as thick as blackberries for my opinion, I think I shall take warning by the Indian judge Macaulay refers to, whose decisions were received with applause until on an unlucky day he gave his reasons for them, and I shall maintain a discreet and masterly silence."

We may judge that Mr. Furness's reasons for his opinion were based on sound logic. As has been remarked before, his powers for exhaustive research were marvelous. He passed whole evenings search-ing for a single phrase. " I remember that I once went through every page of Ben Jonson, and there are nine volumes in Gifford's edition, in search of a single line — and I got it." This is the type of

209

scholar that is so rare in America. Either we have not the patience or the power of compelling ourselves to believe that apparently trivial matters are large matters, after all, if we desire to have a thing perfect.

Mention has been made of the calm, quiet life which Mr. Furness led in his beautiful fire-proof library codifying the Shakespearean material. Even there sorrow found him out, however, for his wife, his sister, and his daughter (all dearly beloved) passed away before him. Though we may note a sadder fall to his words after these griefs, he yet retained his whimsicality to the very end. He was naturally an optimistic man in his daily life, although so much may not be said for his inner spiritual searchings. He believed, and yet he was uncertain. A small doubt bit him like an adder at times. Just as when he had been the head of the Seybert Commission he could find no ground for believing that any one had ever in any way returned from the grave, so in thinking of death itself his logical mind could not but admit that there was no proof of anything beyond. " Isn't there enough faith to go round? " he writes to Charles Eliot Norton. Perhaps there wasn't for him, but something fine took its place, and that was a sturdy belief in the earth itself and the Law that makes most things for the best.

Such a man is unusual in American life. He was not a genius; neither was he a great critic. He *was* a great scholar. In a nation that is less than two hundred years old great scholars are not the rule, and blind patriotism cannot cause good scholars to suffer a sea change into such phœnixes. The great scholar presupposes a mellowed, time-honored background and a cultural atmosphere that is the slow growth of time, and not the instant manufacture of the desire. But Mr. Furness reached that proud height, and it does us no good to speculate as to whether or not the English tradition had touched him. We may guess that it did, but he was essentially American at heart, in spite of the subject he studied all his life. He did not possess the reticence of the Englishman. He was always willing and eager to share his joy and ardor with others. His letters read almost like a diary, for he wrote voluminously, and from them practically every important phase of his life may be reconstructed. He loved small chat, and some of his paragraphs are literary causeries of indubitable charm. Here we may say with absolute confidence that the letters are the man.

A DARTMOOR CYCLE

A DARTMOOR CYCLE

ONE must go back to Thomas Hardy to find the fountain-head of that admirable genre of the English novel in which a few square miles of agricultural territory are fashioned into a stage for elemental action. Wessex is, of course, a world in itself, and upon its dark Egdon Heath and through the streets of its villages and towns and over its farmlands move the varying figures who typify all life. Wind and rain and dark soil mold character and guide destinies. The locale becomes a motif that sounds unceasingly through all the shriller music of mortal passions. There is a dark strength in these books, an atmosphere suggestive of Greek tragedy at times. How much the intimate suggestion of region has fortified the characters or how much the meticulous delineation of character has brought the region into a paramount position are engrossing matters for critical analysis. Both are so inextricably interwoven that it is difficult to say. But it is manifest that an intimate knowledge of the heart and soul of a small portion of territory adds an intensity and concentrated strength to fiction that is not to be found in books wherein the scenes depicted are not the result of specialized study. Thomas Hardy has made a portion of England peculiarly his own for all time. It was but natural that other writers, following the precedent established by Hardy, should stake off other parts of England for themselves. The result has been a deal of excellent writing, but no figure of sufficient importance to place beside the author of the Wessex novels. Sheila Kaye-Smith has adopted Sussex for her own; Eden Phillpotts and John Trevena have taken Dartmoor; and, of course, there are the series of Five Towns novels by Arnold Bennett which picture life in the dreary pottery districts of Staffordshire.

The publication of " Children of Men " by Eden Phillpotts, however, brings his name immediately to the fore for consideration, and this is well, for he is a type illustrating both the virtues and the vices of the regional novelist. " Children of Men " suggests many things. It suggests an author who is, at his best, the nearest approach to Hardy, and who is, at his worst, an exemplar of how dreary a certain type of fiction may be. It is also an additional volume to the series of Dartmoor fictions which Mr. Phillpotts imagined he had completed with " Widecombe Fair " back in 1913. " Children of

Men " may be regarded as a postscript to that series. When " Widecombe Fair " was published Mr. Phillpotts prefaced it with a declaration of what his intention had been. It had been his purpose to say " yea " to life (he was quoting Nietzsche here) and to picture existence as it actually was, thus escaping the " hell of realism or sentimentality." His purpose was a middle course, and his argument was that man's environment is the story of man. This is not far from the ideas held by Hardy, although Phillpotts possesses none of that uncompromising irony that lifts the Wessex novels (the best of them, that is) to the high plane of tragedy. Mr. Phillpotts never quite touches tragedy, although his attempt to do so is manifest at times. He is of smaller stature and he is cursed by a diffuseness that weakens his best situations. In the preface to " Widecombe Fair " he stated:

" We may incarnate the seasons and set them moving, mighty and magic-fingered, upon the face of the earth, to tell a story laden with unsleeping activities, mysterious negations and frustrations, battles and plots, tragedies and triumphs."

" Children of Men " is also prefaced by a statement. Again repeating that he made it his purpose to say " yea " to life " as it unfolded in this small

217

theatre," Mr. Phillpotts announces the ethical principle upon which he has based his series of Dartmoor novels. He states:

"Given faith that conscious Will is at the helm of human affairs, then a definite attitude must result before the spectacle of humanity; but if the mind be built to accept only unconscious Law as controller, the outlook differs, and a resolute trust may develop in man, as ultimate arbiter of his own destiny. Neither assumption can be proved, or disproved; but the relation of a controlling, guiding Spirit to the Universe lies open to doubt; its subjection to law does not; and building upon this latter certainty, I discovered, in the evolution of the moral principle, full cause for trust and for hope."

Fundamentalists will hardly agree with such an attitude, but they cannot fail to treat with respect its exemplification in the Dartmoor novels. The sincerity of the author can never be in doubt. He is essentially a humanist, and every book that he has written proves it. A brief review of the Dartmoor novels (now that they are completed and it is rumored that they will appear in a definite edition in the near future) may be in order. The first one, "Children of the Mist," appeared in 1899. It is loose in construction and there are times when it drags badly (a fault that may be found with most of the novels), but it carries a surprising sense of actuality and it does reveal the life on the moor. Thereafter hardly a year passed that Mr. Phillpotts did not add a new title to the rapidly growing series. There appears to be no conscious method in the relation of one book to another, but the entire series (with many repetitions) gives the appearance of sounding all the varying habits of life in Dartmoor. The best of the books (if one must be dogmatic and according to the consensus of critical opinions) are " The River," " The Secret Woman," " The Whirlwind," " The Mother," " The Three Brothers," " The Beacon " and " Widecombe Fair." " Children of Men," just published, is finely conceived and appears to be tighter-knit than most of the volumes which have gone before. " Widecombe Fair " stands out as the one book without an ordered plot and with more humor than Mr. Phillpotts had shown before. It is a panorama of the whole life of a village, and it moves with genuine gusto.

The novels in this Dartmoor series are, for the most part, marked by a similarity of tone. There are always graceful and finely conceived descriptions of the natural aspects of Dartmoor, the moorlands, the rivers, the villages. Then there is a series of character-vignettes, various types being outlined.

219

The themes themselves are generally variations upon one theme — the love of two people for another person, the old triangle. Certain faults are generally evident. The nature-descriptions (graceful as they are) do not carry the intensity and strength that they should. And this fault weakens the main purpose of the books — to picture man's environment as the molding influence of man's life. One remembers the tremendous description of Egdon Heath in Hardy's "The Return of the Native," and looks in vain for any such symphonic prelude in Mr. Phillpotts' work. Then, too, in the character-drawing of the Dartmoor natives there is much to be desired. These natives do not quite convince us. One is only too aware that it is Mr. Phillpotts talking most of the time and that the opinions broached are quite often beyond the mental equipment of farm hands and even small farmers. One feels differently about Hardy's people. They, too, are exaggerated at times, and there is an element of broad comedy in some of them that rings rather hollow, but they do carry conviction. Perhaps it rests in the abounding vitality of the author. There is nothing of the scholar about Hardy when it comes to fictional treatment; the smoke of the midnight lamp never discolored his pages. With

Mr. Phillpotts one feels a definite talent that is obviously the result of scholarship. His natives are created, for the most part, in his study and not adventured upon in their native habitat. Perhaps one reason for this is that the author always has his thesis in mind. He must fit his types to it.

And yet it would be invidious to cavil too much at these Dartmoor characters. There is a delightful touch upon them. They may not be altogether real, but they are sufficiently vitalized to illustrate how far beyond many characterizations they are. In " Children of Men," for instance, the character of Jacob Bullstone, breeder of dogs and successful farm owner, is developed with a high degree of verisimilitude. One knows Jacob, hard-headed, lacking in imagination, absurdly aware of his importance as a husband and expectant of docility and absolute obedience from his wife, Margery. And how delightful and yet tragic Margery is. Brought up in a smug, narrow-minded, cruel family of The Chosen Few, an almost fanatic religious sect, she should have freedom, a life of her own. Yet she goes willingly and worshipfully to Jacob. The story of her married life and the vicissitudes of her children is finely woven, and with a depth of seriousness that is almost new in the Dartmoor series. It is a fitting postscript and one that may well end the Dartmoor novels in a blaze of glory.

It is obvious that Mr. Phillpotts pins his faith to this series as the source of his future fame. He was wise to do so, for the other things which he has done are of but small moment. He will never be of that great band, the foremost writers of fiction in England, but it is safe to say that he will occupy a lesser place for quite some time to come. He does not have the strength and fierceness of John Trevena, another writer of Dartmoor tales, but he does have larger elements of popularity. Trevena will never be widely read; there is something forbidding in his books. One is glad to have read them; Trevena will have a small audience, always eager to sample the hard-rock-like magic of such books as " Granite " and " Furze," but the audience will be limited. Mr. Phillpotts should possess a larger group of readers, for his narrative vein is more facile.

If any search is to be made for the prime reason why Mr. Phillpotts falls short of the high station toward which he so patently aims, it may perhaps be stated in one word — inspiration. He lacks inspiration, and never once in any of the Dartmoor novels does the reader feel or experience that fine lifting urge that betrays genius in the writer. It is

222

talent that Mr. Phillpotts displays, talent of a high quality which has directed him toward those things which he can do best. The main flaw in his work is a tendency toward wordiness. There is hardly one of the Dartmoor novels which could not have been improved by the excision of many words and the abrupt tightening of situations. His style, at its best, is a leisurely exposition, an unhurried presentation of character by means of the building up of small situations. Gradually the character outlines himself or herself by means of many situations and conversations. Character impinges upon character and a community life gradually evolves. All of these personages are hard-working, rather-frustrated people. Sometimes they do not know their own flaws and unfortunate situations, and at other times they do. Mr. Phillpotts, from a rapid analysis, appears to draw men better than women.

It is the thoughtfulness behind his books that makes it necessary to take Mr. Phillpotts seriously. It is obvious that he has meditated deeply and long on life and that he is anxious to communicate his convictions to the world at large by means of his fictions. One gathers that he is an essential optimist, that he believes the law by which men travel is a steadily ascending one, that the late war was not a retrogression, but a temporary lapse, a momentary aberration. Life goes upward in a steadily ascending arc.

Dartmoor is a peculiarly fine locale for such an undertaking as Mr. Phillpotts has set himself. It is a mountainous country, full of tors and craggy hills, shrouded with mists, set like a tableland in the middle of pleasant Devonshire. The natives are different from those in the lower valleys. They have more to contend with, and it may be guessed that fate tries them much harder than it does city dwellers. It is to be regretted that Mr. Phillpotts did not employ a greater realism in picturing his types, that he did not seek them out instead of creating them in his study. But as it is, he has created a body of work that should give a high degree of pleasure to many readers for years to come.

VAN GOGH AND GOD

VAN GOGH AND GOD

JULIUS MEIER-GRAEFE'S " Vincent van Gogh " is creative biography in the rarest sense of the word. The book moves like a poem, a highly intellectualized poem that is yet vibrant with the impulses of life. Beneath the sliding cadences of exquisite sentences (the credit for which, perhaps, should go to the translator, John Holroyd Reece), the figure of a man reveals itself, grows to more than life-stature and eventually stands as a typification of a certain art-urge. Yet, on second thought, Vincent van Gogh was more than an art-urge; he was a life-urge, a febrile gesture of the intangible kindliness implicit in existence. In a certain sense, he was the slave of love, and because he was so a further perspective reveals him as a master of love. He was a saint and he was an *bete humaine*. He was a Solomon of life and he was a madman. He was not an artist primarily, and he deliberately made himself one. He was cruelly callous and he was the very typification of fervent love. Nowhere in modern history is his like to be found, not even in the sinister unity of Paul Gauguin's attitude toward life after the eleven lean

years as a stockbroker. Van Gogh was an anach-
ronism, a throwback to the medieval ages. He
could subject life to his will, and, even with a
crumbling brain, catch bright flashes of divinity.
With Rembrandt and Delacroix for his masters, he
forced himself to master draftsmanship and color
work, gradually evolving a style that is essentially
his own.

He was not a great painter in the larger sense of
that word; he was not as powerful as Gauguin.
But he was unusual, a fanatic striving furiously to
express himself through paint. In spite of the as-
sertions of loosely thinking critics, Van Gogh did
not create a new movement or bring anything particularly new into art. There is nothing in his canvases that may not be found in others, in some of
the Impressionists and neo-Impressionists. He has
been called an Expressionist, but that is a mere
bandying with words. It is true that he was different from his French contemporaries, but it must be
remembered that he was Dutch. The difference is
one of atavistic tendencies and an incoherent draftsmanship that painfully evolved itself. Van Gogh
was peculiarly naive. He could speak of Rembrandt
and Meissonier in the same breath. He could even
suggest collaboration with Gauguin on canvases.

Gauguin was a master of proportion and great design, but his canvases needed " a more generous array of color." He, Van Gogh, would supply this, would paint in the flower beds and the foliage and the fountains. The tremendous laughter of Gauguin split the air.

This vast naiveté was one of the principal aspects of Van Gogh's existence. He was a child, a veritable child at times, vehemently espousing the most quixotic enterprises. This naiveté, we cannot doubt, was but the natural flowering of a mind congenitally religious, spiritual in its implications and tenderly anxious to spread the doctrine of love. Perhaps the madness was always there, lurking behind the passionate indecision of the mind, a hereditary streak, for it is impossible to conceive of Van Gogh's earlier years as anything but abnormal. He was supersensitive, high-strung, absolutely a fanatic. Dates are but the meagre subterfuges of Time, points that arrest the mind for a moment, but which are nearly meaningless. Life is a succession of movements that originate in deeply hidden impulses, and one may better examine the career of Van Gogh by considering it a matter of movements than of dates. These movements were all, more or less, religious, although it is only the first one that is quite vitally

229

concerned with religion itself. The prelude to this
first movement was but a setting of the spiritual
stage. This prelude includes Van Gogh the boy,
deeply immersed in religious thought and bent upon
a career in the Church.

Van Gogh the dreamer as an art gallery clerk in
The Hague, Van Gogh the impassioned would-be
savior swearing with his brother Theo beside the
old mill at Rijswijk to strive all his life for good,
and Van Gogh the lover. Love flung him abruptly
upon religion again. It was while he was a clerk in
the London branch of Goupil's that he met Ursula.
His failure to win her emphasized in his brooding
nature the fact that he must be a better man if he
was to deserve love. He lost his position and became a sort of assistant preacher in a Methodist
school in Isleworth. Later he went to Amsterdam
to study theology, and there can be no doubt but
what he was more concerned with the emotional side
of it than the theological. In 1878 he was in the
desolate coal mining village of La Borinage preaching to the simple people. Of course, this first movement of his strange life was to end disastrously, for
Van Gogh was an intellect alien to rules. He lived
a Christlike existence, giving his clothes to the very
poor, mingling intimately with them. The Church

authorities in Brussels were convinced that he
cheapened himself, and after less than two years'
preaching he was given notice that he was desired
no longer. So ended the first movement.

While Van Gogh stayed on in his black hole at
La Borinage enduring the disdain of his disap-
pointed family, the second movement slowly came
to birth. No one can properly understand Van
Gogh's art without a realization of the heart-sick
days in La Borinage while he was figuring out life
for himself. The second movement is one of faltering advance, many shifts of methods, starvation,
incessant toil at drawing and a slow assimilation of
fundamentals. Always he had the sturdy friendship
of his brother Theo to help him forward. Without
Theo he would have actually perished of starvation.
This storm and stress period carried him to various
places, to The Hague, to Brussels. During it came
a second love-crisis and so, too, came the affair with
Sien, the woman of the streets. There were various
teachers who helped him, among them Mauve, the
painter. Always before him loomed the unattain-
able beauty of Rembrandt and Delacroix. His work
was dirty, muddy, badly drawn, but behind it was a
driving force, something that caused Theo to have
faith in him and to send him money.

Although Van Gogh walked through the mud of Life, he carried his spirit securely high above it all. It may seem like an anomaly, but through the careful and beautiful exposition of Meier-Graefe the reader witnesses the evolution of Van Gogh's soul. Although he had now taken to painting, he never was an artist in the true sense of the word, for that bespeaks a bending of ideas to technique. Van Gogh did nothing of the sort. He fashioned, or attempted to fashion, technique to his ideas, and the ideas were the same which he possessed as a young preacher. It was the same Van Gogh expressing himself through a new medium. Thus we see that Van Gogh was a spiritual gesture, feebly revealed at times, but always dynamic, always with one end in view. It was love, love alone, that consumed his nights and days, that moved the hand with the brush or quill. This second movement of faltering experimentation came to an end when Van Gogh went to Paris.

There he was no longer the ugly, red-haired freak, the scarecrow of a man animated by mad fancies. He was an artist, contemptuously observed, but nevertheless recognized as a being with ideas. Paris did many things for him. It brought light into his heretofore muddy canvases. It introduced him to impressionism. It gave him museums in which to ramble and study great masterpieces. Best of all, it brought him into contact with Gauguin. The writer sets down the phrase " best of all " advisedly, for in spite of the tragedy that was to happen at Arles it cannot be doubted but what Van Gogh and Gauguin were the two men most fated in all the world to meet. Among these Parisian artists, Gauguin, Seurat, Signac, Lautrec — men who were in some measure reaping what Manet had sowed — Van Gogh was a delightful rudeness. It was a rudeness of a mind, a lack of culture that imbibed much from these more polished figures. He did not quite swing into the tradition, but he was influenced. It strengthened his art intellectually, for it increased his mental range, but it weakened his painting. He tried to be an Impressionist and he could not — he was Van Gogh. A lifeless quality crept into his landscapes; spontaneity was absent. Even his color, which had perceptibly lightened, suffered. Under the influence of Seurat he became almost a neo-Impressionist. But this could not last, and the real Van Gogh, bound by no rules, broke through. During this period came the idea of the co-operative business which Theo was to head. It fizzled out miserably and Paris began to pall on Van Gogh.

The countryside was in his blood; he never was really of the town. It was in February, 1888, that he went to Arles and embarked upon that last spiritual movement that was to end only with his death at Auvers.

Article after article has been written about the Arles period. No one who has studied Gauguin is ignorant of it. But here, for the first time, is Van Gogh's side of it. From the first he wanted Gauguin to come and live with him. Gauguin, who was at Pont-Aven, was not particularly pleased at the thought. The period of time between that when Van Gogh settled in Arles and the day that Gauguin arrived was the happiest in Van Gogh's life. It was a period of peace and constant painting, a fury of work. It is futile to conjecture how things would have turned out had Gauguin never come. One thing is certain, and that is that the germ of madness must have been latent in Van Gogh. The brain had been taxed too severely; it had revolved in and in upon itself and had painfully acquired all the conclusions that animated it by a dogged persistence and exertion. Gauguin merely precipitated the tragedy that was bound to happen.

The influence that Gauguin exerted upon Van Gogh, however, was enormous. To the Dutchman he was a Master, the great teacher, the wise and omniscient dispenser of marvelous truths.* Van Gogh fairly worshipped him. The somewhat saturnine, scoffing nature of Gauguin was exactly the opposite to that of Van Gogh, who was trusting, loving, mentally inferior. There can be no doubt that Van Gogh hoped to convert Gauguin from his scepticism and to a greater faith in men, for the preacher was still strong in Van Gogh. He clung persistently to his illusions, and Gauguin's irony pained him more than it shook his faith. During the time they lived together it is certain that Gauguin improved the painting of Van Gogh by judicious advice. His personality impinged upon the weaker, more trusting man.

The rest of Van Gogh's life may be told in a paragraph. His rages with Gauguin increased. One night they went to a brothel where a little brunette, pretending that Van Gogh was a bear, demanded his ear. It was a joke, and all laughed. The next day at lunch he flung a wine-glass at Gauguin, who dodged it and flung Van Gogh into the street. Gauguin prepared to leave Arles, and only changed his mind a day later when Van Gogh, humbly apologizing, begged him to stay. That night Gauguin, walking after dinner, heard steps behind him and turned to find Van Gogh with a glittering knife. " Vincent," he called. " Yes, Master," said the madman, and turned and ran back home. Gauguin went to an inn to sleep. About midnight a small package was brought to the brothel for the little brunette. Opening it, she found a human ear that had been slashed off. In the morning Gauguin, strolling to the house where he lived with Van Gogh, found an excited crowd before it. Vincent was lying asleep in the blood-stained bed, his head swathed in bandages. Theo came and Vincent was taken to a hospital. After his recovery he went back to Arles, and, daily, crowds gathered before his house shouting, " Fou-roux! Fou-roux! " One day in spring he attempted to address this crowd of baiters, and, being violently interrupted, he flung canvas after canvas at them. The boys stuck their heads through the broken frames, and Van Gogh screamed and bellowed like a dog. Eighty-one citizens of Arles petitioned the removal of the madman. What followed was a series of mad attacks interspersed through a period of swift painting. Van Gogh first was placed in the Asylum of Saint Remy and later in charge of Dr. Gachet at Auvers. The last scene was played out there. One day in a mad fit Van Gogh shot himself through the stomach. To the very last he painted, and some of his best canvases belong to this period of intermittent madness. It was Theo, the faithful brother, who, sitting by the dying man's bed, uttered the painter's valedictory. He said:

"Yes, Vincent, you have had more than your share of misery, and your misery has become the happiness of your pictures. There have been few good moments in which you were allowed to approach your fellows; there were no arms to wrap you round, and even I, perhaps, was not allowed to love you. But your pictures are warm embraces. Many people tread the middle path between suffering and joy, and they stroll through the world, grinning inanely or more often sighing, and finally, they stumble round a dark corner, which makes them even smaller than they were before, and they leave behind them nothing but a heap of sighs and a little futile laughter. But you have traced eternal furrows and your agony will quench the thirst of coming generations. The greater your suffering has been, the mightier have been the joyous footsteps of your journey. Plowing furrows has been your destiny, and you strode across the fields like a sower. Think of the days you have been sowing; there are few in which you have been idle. The expression of your face no doubt has grown distorted; was it anguish or the mark of honest labor? The bread you have eaten has been hard, your fellows have

237

been hard to you, and hard has been the treatment God has meted out to you every day of your life. But your work, the structure that you leave behind you, is as firm as the hardness you experienced. When your heart has ceased to beat within your bosom, it will throb in your pictures."

Van Gogh died in the early hours of July 29, 1890. He was thirty-seven years old.

Much has been omitted in the retelling here. Those final utterances of Van Gogh from his death-bed, the intimate details of the existence of Gauguin and Van Gogh together, much of the development of the various aspects of the painter's life, including his thoughts on art and the progress of his genius, are to be found in the book, and they are best read there in the framework which Meier-Graefe has so beautifully created for them. Together with the one hundred and two excellent reproductions of his work, the matter gives an admirable and, it cannot be doubted, truthful picture of Vincent Van Gogh, both the outer and the inner man. This is a book of the soul as well as one of the body. It is the spirit that is traced so carefully and poetically from its first religious passions to the high mad passion of the deathbed. It is medieval in spirit.

This fine literary achievement should do many

excellent things for the fame of Van Gogh. It quite removes him from the class of the esthetic innovator (although in a certain sense, of course, he was that) and places him among the mystics of art. It was always life in contact with spiritual aspects that moved him, and draftsmanship and color were but secondary to this paramount objective. He becomes tne touching example of the man who, born with only the spiritual ardor, forges his own weapons in the white-hot crater of life. He came without advantages and he wrested knowledge from the palette. Without money and proper teachers, often led astray because he was forced to think things out for himself, he yet perfected the method best adapted to his scheme of things for self-expression. His work was done when he died; there was no need for him to live longer.

THE REVIEWER IN MID-CHANNEL

THE REVIEWER IN MID-CHANNEL

SIR ARTHUR WING PINERO once wrote a play entitled " Mid-Channel," which was concerned with that period of married life when the couple grew restless and dissatis‍fied with each other. The glamor of the honeymoon had worn away. A mutual existence had revealed the faults of husband and wife, the little things that irritate. Both wondered if they might not have done better. So existence became as choppy and uncertain as the middle of the English Channel. Successful marriages weather this period and sail into the calm waters of experience and tolerance. Unsuccessful ones founder. I imagine the same must be true of veteran book reviewers. They reach a mid-channel where they are overwhelmed with the futility of their existence. The same meretricious books appear and the reviewer writes down the same empty phrases. The reviewer wonders if he might not have done better if he had taken up plumbing or got a job in a hand laundry.

All of which, perhaps, indicates that I have reached thirty years of age, given up the Great

American Book as a joke, did not rest through my vacation, and need a change of diet. But I feel that it is more than this. I feel that it is time to take stock, deliberate, and reach conclusions. In other words, I must end a period. I must shake out the vast rag-bag of odds and ends that have gathered throughout twelve years (bits of Pater, phrases of Symons, theories of De Gourmont, backward glances at Matthew Arnold), sort the few things of value from the pile, calmly tie up the remainder into a neat parcel, and take it out to the middle of Williamsburg Bridge, say (a figurative Williamsburg Bridge), drop it over the side, and return with as innocent an expression as a reviewer can register upon his supposedly somewhat sinister countenance. Perhaps the parcel will float out into the Atlantic Ocean. Perhaps it will cross that vast expanse of water (unvexed by literary reviews) and be flung up on the shore of Merrie England. Perhaps Robert Lynd or J. C. Squire or Edward Garnett will see it and pick it up. And in this way I will disrupt English literary criticism. I am very sure that in the past England has done the same to us. Many and many a parcel of discarded theories has washed upon our native shores. Anyway, I have been carrying this load too long. I have had too

many convictions. I have not been inconsistent
enough. While others have been courageously
writing criticism I have been timidly writing reviews. The distinction is obvious, as even Professor
Brander Matthews will admit. It is unbearable.
I must do something about it.

And so the realization becomes clear that I have
reached the end of a period, and to end it properly
I must discover exactly what I think about people
who write poetry. I must discover what I think
about the people whose books I have been reviewing
in a somewhat easy-going and comatose state for
the past decade or more. And I must look a bit
beyond them and ferret out the enthusiasms that
made me essentially a reviewer of poetry. It is a
truism that all things move in cycles, and it is quite
possible that the mind of the critic (to which I lay
no claim, dear scoffers) eventually reaches the place
from which it made its first rash advance.

I think that it was in 1905 or 1906 that I came
to life and suddenly observed that there were a
great many books to read which were just being
written. As to authentic values, any student may
turn back to the Sahara-like expanse of American
letters during those years and judge for himself.
We were living on the fag-end of an old tradition,

although, of course, it never occurred to me that a
new era might be about to knock on the gate. My
juvenile capacities could not embrace the writing on
the wall. I could hear the creaking of the rotting
pile at times, but how was I to know that it pre-
figured the sudden crashing down of stately old
edifices? Before those years 1905 or 1906 I had
hugged the delusion that the only books worth reading were those that had been written by men long
since dead. I knew that I wanted to be a poet
(much to the disgust of my boyhood friends), and
perhaps it was this desire that led me to open the
pages of Jessie B. Rittenhouse's "The Younger
American Poets." I can understand now what an
adventure that book was. Her very title postulated
something that was doubted. She was crying in the
Great Thebaid of America, and there were few to
listen. She published her book in 1904. It was
sublime. Whether or not she proved her case I do
not know. In some cases I am afraid she did not.
The book had its omissions, but I did not observe
them, and there was no reason to expect Mrs.
Rittenhouse to observe them. She included poets
that are today nonentities, and she left out, for instance, Mr. Edwin Arlington Robinson, who had,
I believe, published three books when her volume

was written and whose sterling qualities were recognized by Theodore Roosevelt in *The Outlook* in 1905. He, too, was a prophet.

It is interesting to observe some of the names which Mrs. Rittenhouse considered in her volume — interesting to me, at least, for I cut my poetic teeth upon them, if such an outrageous phrase may be allowed one who is thoroughly shameless. Who remembers Frederick Lawrence Knowles today? Yet the charm of his " Love Triumphant," somewhat faint, to be sure, lingers with me still. I can even repeat that poem beginning —

> Helen's lips are drifting dust;
> Ilion is consumed with rust;
> All the galleons of Greece
> Drink the ocean's dreamless peace.

And Mary McNeill Fenollosa and Gertrude Hall and Arthur Upson? *Ou sont les neiges d'antan?* All of these poets had their importance then. But how sad and true it is that most of these " younger American poets " stopped right there and failed to reach the stature of " older American poets "! What happened to them? What delayed them? Was it because they were playing on violins that were steadily crumbling to dust in their hands? Were they merely spinning out a tradition that had already blown thin?

247

There was no furor for poetry in America fifteen years ago. Perhaps we were resting up from the spiritual exhaustion of the Yellow Nineties. And yet I am not inclined to think that that era had much influence upon us, if we except such isolated examples as " Mam'selle New York," the organ of Messrs. Huneker, Vance Thompson, Percival Pollard, and a few kindred souls. It may be possible that Pegasus was hibernating, presumably in the Cave of Æolus. Certainly he burst forth with rushing winds not so long thereafter. Those years of barrenness were years of expectation and gestation. It was the lull before the storm. For the lovers of poetry, and they appeared few enough, it was all expectancy. For the poets themselves, and they were fewer still, it was all gestatory. For some it was not even gestatory. Miss Millay, for instance, was possibly falling down and bumping her nose and Miss Welles was probably crooning to her doll. Mrs. Wylie was but an eaglet in the nest, and Mr. Untermeyer, it may be suspected, was smoking his first cigarette behind the fence. Mr. Masters was undoubtedly beginning the years of arduous practice that were to end, possibly to his own extreme bewilderment, in " Spoon River Anthology." Most of the younger generation were just crawling out of their cradles.

Still, there was Mr. Clinton Scollard, who came riding in with the wind from the desert, Khamsin! and Mr. Richard Watson Gilder pouring forth his mellifluous golden notes from the office of the "Century." And what a group of minor figures! Frank Dempster Sherman, Lloyd Mifflin, Virginia Woodward Cloud, John B. Tabb, Madison Cawein, Richard Burton, Charles G. D. Roberts, and a dozen others! They were fine — then.

In such an era I put Wordsworth and Keats and Longfellow on the back shelf and began to wonder about the values of poetry. I could feel the lack that steadily grew into a prodigious ache of a great figure. Of course, we pinned our faith to various writers. There was Mr. Ridgely Torrence, to whose genius I still pin my faith. It has been pinned there for fifteen years, but hope is deathless. Bliss Carman was a man to ponder about, but the greater shadow of Richard Hovey, then but lately dead, somewhat obscured him. I could never read Carman without thinking of Hovey and going back to the three series of "Songs from Vagabondia." Edwin Arlington Robinson, a strange, solitary figure, was writing poetry practically as mature as the work he puts forth today, but somehow I did not discover him. Neither did anyone else, for that matter. And there were Louise Imogen Guiney, George E. Santayana, Josephine Preston Peabody, George E. Woodberry, who ate of the laurel, Alice Brown, and Harriet Monroe. It can hardly be asserted that any one of them fulfilled the prophecies of their disciples. Perhaps it was the atmosphere of America; perhaps they merely reached the limits of their endeavors and could go no further. I know that most of them will pardon me for writing of them in a past tense, but it is a fact that they belong to an era which does not exist. It is not their fault. Some of them were excellent poets as poets go. It is my conviction that their lost vogue is occasioned by a new intellectual spirit, an eager and youthful curiosity that is impatient of the fagends of past periods. It was in the fringe of a dying period that I first started to write reviews. With bowed head I acknowledge that I matured too soon. I should have been born five years later. I have been trying to straddle two periods — one of youthful enthusiasms, the other of mature reflections. And that is why I have reached mid-channel. The two attitudes of mind do not jibe.

I have reached a point of time. I am trembling upon the perilous brink of thirty, and I must wave my hand to sweet sixteen. It is impossible to go back now. And it is hard to go forward. But no longer will I sing "Blue Bell" to the accompaniment of the banjo or observe the balloon-like puffs upon my sister's sleeves. The Sunday bicyclists have gone with the Gibson pompadours. College ices have become sundaes and petticoats have gone the way of the wind. The dear breathless days of expectation are over, and I must sit in the shade of the sheltering palm (ah, "Florodora"!) and patiently await a new crop of them. I am foolishly aware that if I am permitted to reach the ripe age of forty (by irate authors) I shall write an article bewailing the disappearance of the past decade's convictions. I shall do the same at fifty, and so on, *ad infinitum.* It is the pleasantest sort of essay to write, anyway, for one alternately smiles and sighs while inditing it.

O tempora! O mores! I shall be reading Charles Lamb again and bellowing at the quips of my Uncle Toby. I shall even wipe the dust from Samuel Richardson's "Clarissa Harlowe" with the anticipation of really finding out what is in the book from which I learned to read. But I shall not open it, after all. By the time I get that far a new batch of poetry will arrive via the parcels post (in the old days we had to go to the office to get it) and I shall be formulating a new set of theories.

It appears to me that these scattered thoughts prove only one thing — once a reviewer, always a reviewer. Mid-channel once past, the reviewer is safe in the sheltered harbor of mature thought. His convictions may rise about him like high peaks and promontories and shut some of the vistas away, but perhaps his limitations are good. At least he knows thoroughly what is in the bay. And it is easy enough to sight new ships. The peaks and promontories may be climbed. Balboa is a case in point.

MY EDUCATION

MY EDUCATION

MY EDUCATION

I.

THE old library at Springfield, Massachusetts (now long since torn down) was a pleasantly informal, quaint-looking red-brick building with all its treasures easily accessible to the chance wanderer. One was not required to painstakingly look up a book in the card-index, write its name on a slip of paper, and then wait an unconscionable time until it was produced by a scornful young (or old) lady. One just wandered among the book-stacks themselves and browsed in that delightful loneliness that should surround every reader in a library. There was no efficiency here. One just stumbled onto unexpected treasures, blew the dust from them and then sank upon a stepping-stool for higher shelves (not selves, necessarily — the Restoration dramatists were always high up) or at a small table, and imbibed lusty draughts of knowledge. It was utterly delightful. While approaching the library one achieved a certain state of mind. The street was sunny, plenty of green lawns met the gaze, several church-spires

solemnly denoted " the peace that passeth understanding," and, best of all, Augustus St. Gaudens's
statue of " The Puritan " posed before the red-brick
building, one gnarled hand on his cane and the other
supporting the huge Bible under his arm. He was
always just about to step off his pedestal, but he
never got quite that far. Though sparrows would
chatter about his hat and small urchins would climb
up betwixt his legs and view the universe from that
proud perch, he never altered his expression. Observing the world from the square-toed shoes of
" The Puritan " probably connotes a symbolism, but
it is doubtful that any of the urchins (from whom I
was but lately graduated) saw it in that light. For
them the virtues of the statue centered in a flowing
cape that protected them from chance showers and
made a good hiding place. As I say, it was all quite
delightful.

But all this, as Mr. Hudson would say, is long
ago and far away. It was in that dim prehistoric
period when the eohippus had ceased to exist, but
before the Great War. Why, it was as far back as
the days when " Blue Bell " was the *piéce de resistance* of the hurdy-gurdies, bicycles were still in
vogue, " Teddy " was President, and my sister's
hair lurched unsteadily upon her head in a coiffure

popularly known (at least, to us youngsters) as the
flopping pompadour. Dear, dear, how long ago it
was! "I feel chilly and grown old." In such a
milieu I pursued the even tenor of my way. That
way mostly led to the library, where I would pass
the greater part of the day in an unsystematic per-
usal of books. There was a certain perverse pleasure in jumping from the "Roxburgh Ballads" to
"Urn-Burial," and from thence to "Walden." New
wonders constantly revealed themselves in the most
unlikely corners. The opening of a broken cover
would reveal the Plays of Massinger; an undeciph-
erable title would turn out to be a reprint of "The
Tatler." It will be observed that I kept away from
new books. They were in another room promi-
nently displayed upon clean, dusted shelves, easily
accessible to all. The very, very new fiction cost
two cents a day. How silly to be forced to pay two
cents for George Barr McCutcheon, for instance,
while John Donne, poems, sermons and all, cost
absolutely nothing, and, being non-fiction, could be
carted away as a sort of contemptuous free gift with
"Graustark." I passed the new fiction with becoming hauteur. I preferred prowling in the dark
corners; the dust of Time literally enveloped my
finds. How Columbus-like I felt when, pouring

257

through an old tome spattered with long s's, I would chance upon such lines as "A bracelet of bright hair about the bone." How the B's buzzed in my head. It was not, therefore, until I had digested many an ancient and rakish-looking volume that I began to speculate upon the possibility that literature was still being written. I have explained elsewhere in print how the discovery of Jessie Rittenhouse's " The Younger American Poets " started me gorging on contemporary letters. I put the Iliad away; dust began to close Helen's eye. It was time to come forth from the tomb.

But the smell of old buckram was upon my spirit as well as my hands. I had reveled in two or three old literatures until my mind was like a rag-bag filled with variously-hued bits. I had employed no reason in my reading; I had acquired no single thing wholly. I had just dived here and there in the wine-dark sea, and often enough I came up speedily for air and dove in that particular region no more. I knew a bit of this and a bit of that, one man's books and another man's chapter, but I had co-ordinated nothing. It was impossible for me to formulate any logical premises or convictions. I adored books. I loved to read. Certain things moved me mightily and other efforts left me cold. Quite suddenly I

destroyed all my joy in reading by a cursed realization that I must begin to think. I didn't want to
think. I wanted just to read and let the books do
what they would with me. But the reservoir became
full; the mixture started to react; I began to boil
inside.

Now do you see what happened? In an old red
building set amidst the most delightful greenery,
with a church next door, and St. Gaudens's statue
on the lawn, I began to boil inside, letting the steam
escape in botchy essays, echoing poems, inconsistent
monstrous conversations. I talked to everybody,
including the letter-carrier and " The Puritan."
The letter-carrier did not have time to listen, but
" The Puritan " was grimly patient, although there
must have been times when he experienced a wild
desire to step from his pedestal and flee hastily down
State Street, Bible and all. But who would listen
to me? Who would converse with me? Who would
argue about life and letters and love and philosophy
and walruses and kings until the moon smouldered
down like a consumed candle and the morning stars
began to sing? I was as dithyrambic as that! The
answer was, Nobody! There was no Younger
Generation in those days. What should have been
the Younger Generation apparently had been born

with whiskers and morals and all the usual appendages of maturity. What we now know as The Younger Generation was growing up, perhaps trying to find somebody who would stand still long enough to engage in argumentation. There *were* older people, of course. But they were very much like " The Puritan " to my untrained observation. They simply did not converse. They did not expect young men to have opinions. They emphasized the fact that one must serve one's apprenticeship to life with becoming silence. They listened and then patronizingly flung me a few assorted judgments. I would have to find people of my own age with whom to talk. Eventually (ring out, wild bells!) I did.

II.

The Younger Generation has been created in some measure by the lack of intelligent conversation. Most Younger Generations crystallize in this way. But heretofore the various generations had slid imperceptibly into one another. Something happened in my nonage. There came a hiatus in the stream of esthetic, ethical and humanistic conversation which, up to that point, had rolled along in an unbroken flood since the first man began to argue with his son. Consequently the tradition broke, the links snapped. Our older intelligentsia created this Frankenstein's monster which is, after all, only a pathetic gesture of self-preservation. There is nothing horrible about the Younger Generation. The tocsin of revolt is more of an antitoxin than anything else. It is a defensive proteid. The Younger Generation simply wanted to talk, to know, and then it discovered that it would have to learn for itself. For some strange reason its questions embarrassed the old order. Certain points focussed. Along came the Great War, and in five years as much life had been piled upon the Younger Generation as had been meted out to our elders in fifty years. Such a congestion could not but result in a

261

rush of brains to the head. Extravagances became reasonable developments in a monstrous and extravagant era.

Let me ask two questions which I admit may be answered in several different ways. Why did the chain of tradition break because of the inability of our elders to pass it along to us in conversation? Why couldn't they convince us? And why does an inborn spirit of revolt prevent the Younger Generation from meeting with the past ideals in natural amity? The first question suggests other queries. Did our elders become more self-conscious than *their* fathers in that they could not intelligently pass on the chain unbroken, or were we the first generation to refuse to accept our culture on bended knees from patronizing lips? It is patent that our fathers either could not or would not meet us on a common ground. They would not say to us, " You have minds of your own, and if the transcendentalism of Emerson seems to you a hollow subterfuge in this year, 19—, there is no reason for you to swallow it without cavil or examination." Instead of this, they enunciated, " It has been examined by us. It is all right. Take it. We liked it. It did good service in 1880. We believe in it." " We don't " chorused the Younger Generation. " We have been applying

262

it to our own era and it doesn't hold water." Naturally a new war was on. Where did we get the courage to say, " We don't "? Was all this merely because the older tradition had ossified and was nothing but a cold, heartless stone for us who were begging for bread? If this is so, why had it not happened in the past to other generations? What devilish impudence animated our defiant tongues with such vigor?

Now the Younger Generation is not a miracle. It is but a recrudescence of combativeness. Every era has its Younger Generation, its group of callous young heretics who shift the progress of thought into new channels. But the tradition has persisted in the past in spite of this. Styles have changed; moods have veered; new discoveries and science have shifted ancient aspects. Still the tradition has carried on. The old band-wagon has been redecorated, repainted a hundred times, but it was propelled by the same old wheels. The difference today is not one of style, but of substance. The very body of letters is being transformed into another thing. The tradition has broken because the Younger Generation insist upon dipping their pens in life instead of ink, because they approach existence in cerebral terms instead of esthetic mannerisms. They demand freeaom, freedom of thought, of technique, of application, of exposition. They are wise and unwise. Their goal is a great one, but their multitudinous approaches are often ridiculous in the extreme. Let all this be admitted. The Younger Generation desires to creep into the mystic heart of life, that hidden place beyond good and evil, and it will not shut its eyes to the filth through which it must travel. For the first time it ignores the ethical application.

Now just what is it that arouses such anger in our elders? It cannot be a new genre of letters wholly, for such things have been known to happen before, and the tradition has been but fractured, never broken. As I see it, one great cause of difference (and really an old one, as the history of letters shows) lies in our loss of respect (or rather worship) for the thrice honored Sacred Lamas of Literature. We do not crawl into the temple on humble knees and smack our foreheads on the chancel-rail while the priests (that older generation that has forgotten it was young because it sprang out of the decaying half of the Victorian era) stand pompously by and condescendingly inform us that we are good little boys. Instead of this, we swagger by, a bit vulgar, perhaps, at times, often ineffectual, but certainly biting. The Chosen Ones (mainly self-

chosen) view us with amazement and, waving awed
hands at their deities, exclaim, "You are not like
them!" "Thank God," we reply, or "Thank
Dionysus," or "Thank the Time-Spirit," and continue swaggering. Of course, it really profits us no
more than it does our elders, this swashbuckling and
school-boy contempt. It is merely a vent. No, the
importance of the Younger Generation does not rest
in our histrionics. It is unstable, transient, an orgy
of attitudes, a juggling of barbarous masks, a litur-
gy of boldness. The importance is to be found
elsewhere.

It is to be found (to name one source) in our
readiness to accept living gods. This, I write, in
spite of the ridicule that it will arouse amongst our
elders, and, indeed, some of our contemporaries.
"Living gods," they sneer. "Ah, T. S. Eliot,
James Joyce, Ezra Pound, Sherwood Anderson!"
The laughter should be loud, for that is one of the
chief vents of our elders. But let me attempt an
explanation of what I mean by this. T. S. Eliot,
for instance, may be a great writer or he may be the
prime hoaxer that certain quarters maintain, but that
does not injure the validity of my argument. It is
the word "readiness" in the opening sentence of

this paragraph that I wish to emphasize. Why must a man be dead before he receives that meed of praise and recognition which is, after all, the solitary reward of the literary creator? Why must the opening lines of his hymn of praise be sung to the dull sound of clods upon his coffin? What mortuary spirit is this which constantly asserts that only death releases our self-consciousness and permits us unrestrainedly to praise a splendor that is cold? It is very well to assert that Tennyson, Longfellow, and others were recognized as geniuses during their lifetime. The argument is not valid. They were national institutions, and the public saw their own ideals reflected in them. They were old men, and it is always pleasant to praise old men. Victorianism crowed at itself in the Poet Laureate. Sentimentalism saw its own features in the Germanic sweetness of Longfellow. A code of ethics was worshipped in each man. The public did not go to them; they slid into the public. The mass-mind became an individual in one poet. The Younger Generation stands ready to praise young men, to acknowledge genius in its own day. Would it not be better foolishly to praise thirty men if one among them be a genius? The ill-advised adulation of the other twenty-nine will dim fast enough. But how sweet to

266

realize that we have praised a great talent during its actual lifetime!

Our Elders have been afraid to praise living men for fear that their judgments might be reversed by cold history. Some of these bearded prophets have even asserted that it is impossible to criticise a contemporary. "Nothing is impossible," we reply and go on, using our wits as best we may, acknowledging greatness where we seem to see it, yet not acknowledging it promiscuously. The Younger Generation is as aristocratic in its judgments and as hard to please as any generation that has ever existed.

"Readiness" is the watchword of the Younger Generation. It is eager to praise, eager to experiment, eager even to condemn. Of course, the most banal mistakes are made, but are they not better than this sure-footed walking amongst the tombs which has been and is the practice of our elders? The readiness to remark good work, to expatiate upon it, to argue, to worship, can result in one thing only — a making richer of the soil from which genius springs. After all, achievement is a relative matter. Shakespeare's plays were much more wonderful, miracles, indeed, during his lifetime. Consider his surroundings and the meagerness of his background. How much more wonderful it would have been, then, to have praised him during his lifetime, a gracious gesture which some of his own Younger Generation appears to have made. Therefore, the Younger Generation will maintain its right to march insolently by the Sacred Lamas and constantly show a readiness to admit unusual talent when it imagines or is convinced that it is present. It will praise vigorously, astoundingly sometimes, and it will continue to look for that contemporary atmosphere which must be implicit in the men it praises. One cannot praise living men unless they write living literature, and the methods and ethical quibbles of dead men, however great, cannot be the substance of living literature.

III.

I must return to the old red-brick building in Springfield, Massachusetts. When I declared that something began to boil inside me, that I looked and longed for conversation, it was with the intimation that I was stepping out of an old world into a new. Rather I was looking for a New World which, at that time, did not exist, which, indeed, does not really exist now. But its beauty falls from the air and gives me a hint of what it will be. It is pre-figured in long talks lasting far beyond midnight, and not in conversation about the busts in the Hall of Fame or the crumbled dust in Westminster Abbey. It comes in eager speculations about living writers, in the goals for which they start out on their high, proud, self-sufficient journeys. Most of all, it is hinted at in my readiness to accept with becoming seriousness the serious attempts of those men and women who starkly fly the gonfalons of living literature. " Readiness " and " living literature " are the words which move me most. They, I think, express the Younger Generation. At least, they express one side of its multifarious activities.

St. Gaudens's statue still stands beside a library in Springfield. It is a new library, a beautiful white

269

building given by the Scotch philanthropist, efficient in its system, crammed with great literature. The old brick building has gone, gone with my youth and " Blue Bell " and bicycles and flopping pompadours. And perhaps it is just as well. If I saw it I might try to saunter in and browse amongst those dusty book-stacks, seeking for " The Tatler " and " Urn-Burial " and " The Roxburgh Ballads." And I don't think I should relish that. A cold wind would blow upon me and the dust of more than books would be upon my fingers. The dust of my own youth would be there and I should be an old man. But as it is, I am a young man, riding the wind of a new era that will undoubtedly demolish me. Still, the air is exhilarating. Where I am going I know not, but I am certainly on my way somewhere. I touch hands in which the blood continues to flow, meet eyes that are filled with excitement, and talk — talk incessantly. And in the bright tingling air about me the New World steadily creates itself, Phœnix-like, from the ashes of the old.